Don't get **Saucy** *with me,* **Béarnaise**

Peta Mathias

photographs by
Laurence Belcher

RANDOM HOUSE
NEW ZEALAND LTD

in association with

TVNZ
TELEVISION

PREVIOUSLY WRITTEN BY THE AUTHOR

Fête Accomplie
(Random House, 1995)

Random House New Zealand Ltd
(An imprint of the Random House Group)

18 Poland Road
Glenfield
Auckland 10
NEW ZEALAND

Sydney New York Toronto
London Auckland Johannesburg
and agencies throughout the world

First published 1996

Text © Peta Mathias 1996
Illustrations © Laurence Belcher 1996
The moral rights of the Author have been asserted.

Designed by Graeme Leather
Printed in Hong Kong
ISBN 1 86941 305 9

CONTENTS

Acknowledgements

Deepest gratitude and affection for my clever editor Harriet Allan for encouragement, support and neck massages.

Thanks to Juliet Rogers, managing director of Random House for not only looking at me once but looking at me twice.

Buckets of smiles for Michael Moynahan and Tammy Taylor of Random House for being dedicated, funny and adorable.

Embarrassing feet kissing to Irene Gardiner, producer of *Town & Country* for giving me a break and laughing her head off when a letter of complaint came in about my hair and clothes.

Thanks to Laurence Belcher for the wonderful photos, gin and tonics and sense of humour.

Thanks to Chris Wright for teaching me how to memorise more than two sentences at a time, for always saying, 'It'll do,' when I was brilliant, and for having an easy temperament that I could only aspire to.

Thanks to my brother Paul for providing the goofy title.

Much love to my family and friends who are too perfect.

List of Recipes

Believe it or not, I am in love with people and food in equal parts, so when Irene Gardiner of TVNZ asked me to audition for the 'Taste NZ' food segment on *Town & Country* I thought:

'Can this be true? Can I really be a show off and eat and travel and have them call it a job? Is there a God after all?'

Irene sounded like she was about eighteen on the phone, and I was terribly impressed that someone so young could produce the entire leisure programming for TVNZ. I went in to meet her one fine, sunny afternoon and immediately wondered why she wasn't on the other side of the screen. Irene's good looks appeared only to be exceeded by her brains.

The audition was in the middle of nowhere (Greenhithe), and cats and dogs fell out of the sky along with walls of water. I made a mental note to punish the person who had organised this ridiculous location. Patiently waiting for me were Chris Wright, the producer, and Laurence Belcher, the researcher. I had to do my little food thing outside in the deafening rain sheltered by the patio roof, then interview Laurence about the imaginery pork pies he was importing to New Zealand. By the end of the interview, I told him he could bugger off with his revolting pies and go back to where he came from.

THE HOKIANGA CREW IN A SERIOUS MOOD — FROM LEFT, RICHARD (SOUND), CHRIS (DIRECTOR), LAURENCE (PHOTOGRAPHER). WHO'S THE WOMAN DOING THE QUASIMODO IMPERSONATION?

A few weeks later, I got a call saying I had been short-listed and could I come in for another audition. *Short-listed!* Surely I wasn't going to have to go through this nerve-racking process *again! Mais oui.* Off I trudged to an address in Parnell, this time armed with a few inches of war paint applied by the gorgeous Renée in the TVNZ makeup room. I was asked to interview Judith Taberon of Ramses restaurant. She turned up looking like a million dollars and made the interview so easy for me, I thought I might actually be able to do it on a regular basis. I was to find out that not everyone is as articulate as Judith, in fact, some people would rather be boiled than speak to a camera.

Filming all over New Zealand for *Town & Country* turned out to be a joy in every way — in terms of working with Chris and Laurence, of sourcing fabulous products, meeting great people and spending hours putting together my Zambezi outfits. There's no reason to lower your standards just because you're a simple cook. Everywhere we went, people pressed food on us. No room? Never fear — we'll send it up to you. After every shoot we came home laden with gifts from generous producers.

At the end of the series, Irene organised a cocktail party and I met the other presenters for *Town & Country* for the first time. David Cull told me I had maligned Chris by saying he would eat anything. Apparently, everyone wants to work with Chris because he always knows where the good places are to eat and where the speciality foods are hidden. There were bubbly, *Sushi* Rolls, fried wontons, club sandwiches and baby greens. Irene took one look at the finger food spread out everywhere and said, 'There is not one thing here I can eat. I'm not paying the bill. I want sausage rolls and I'm sick of being penalised for preferring simple food.'

Peta recording a programme voice-over.

I suppose the big revelation for me with 'Taste NZ' was that there is a wealth of regional products in this country and a lot of them never leave their province. There are pockets of people who still cook the ethnic food of their ancestors, and the Asians who have raised the standard and choice of seafood in New Zealand to unimaginable heights. There are tiny, boutique cheese makers making the most mouth-watering cheese, queen scallops that no one knows about except Dunediners, Irish bread that only Christchurchers get to taste, and trout you can only eat if you catch it yourself. We tasted wine in Queenstown that was matured in a huge cave tunnelled out of a mountain and wine that grew out of black rocks. We ate flounder straight out of the Hokianga Harbour and cheesecakes make from Quarg, not to mention home-made *prosciutto* and Mozzarella. And what about mountain oysters? You haven't tasted New Zealand until you've tasted them.

THE FRENCH FARM PICNIC, PRODUCE COLLECTED ON OUR TRAVELS FROM CHRISTCHURCH TO AKAROA.

dunedin

le *Créateur, en obligeant l'homme a manger pour vivre, l'y invite par appétit, et l'en récompense par le plaisir* — the creator, in obliging man to eat to live, invites him by appetite and repays him by pleasure

BRILLAT-SAVARIN

When I said I was going to Dunedin to shoot our first segment of *Town & Country*, my friends immediately divided themselves into two non-negotiable camps:

Camp A — 'Dunedin! How ghastly, you poor thing. The weather's horrible, only dour misfits live there and they eat unspeakable, ignoble things. The food's so terrible they hide it in sheep's stomachs so they don't have to look at it.'

Camp B — 'Dunedin! We're so jealous. The architecture's wonderful — the Athens of the South — the inhabitants amicable and the arts scene is probably the best in New Zealand. Once you've lived in Dunedin you can never live anywhere else.'

I arrived on a sunny, clear November day to be met at the airport by Laurence, our researcher, who drove me to some builder's fantasy in the form of a white, stucco hacienda that clearly thought it was a hotel in Ibiza rather than New Zealand's version of Scotland. I was to discover that all motel rooms in this country are designed to sleep a minimum of thirty-seven people, cater for two people in terms of kitchen utensils and allow for zero people in terms of irons. Having cased our respective joints, downed a gin and tonic and jumped up and down on our beds, Laurence and I, along with our illustrious director Chris, fearlessly set out to brave the streets in search of sustenance. The criteria for deciding on a restaurant were established firmly that evening, and nothing happened in the duration of the series to change this: Laurence will go with the flow; Peta will only eat good food; Chris will eat anything.

In the morning, the Dunedin side of the crew turned up in the persons of John the cameraman and Barrie the sound man. We set out for our first destination in two rental cars and a TVNZ van full of mysterious and magical apparatuses, which John and Barrie artfully arranged all over themselves as the day proceeded. Our first stop was deceptively simple and pleasant — a nice lady called Jane at the 119 Café who made us cheese rolls, a south-of-the-South Island specialty. Cheese rolls are basically a toasted sandwich rolled up. You mix together common-or-garden grated cheese, some minced onion and a dollop of English mustard to a paste. You spread this on square slices of white bread, roll them up and toast them under the grill. My challenging job was to eat a bite of this melting log. Gosh! I thought, this is hard, I'd *much* rather be slaving over a hot stove and losing the battle with stress control. Gentle reader, when I saw the edited cut of this segment I fell into a foetal position and gasped 'NO MORE CLOSE-UPS!'

'Don't be ridiculous,' they said, 'you didn't get the job for your looks.'

I was to be punished for enjoying Jane's cheese roll by being driven straight to the haggis factory. Was ever a more terrifying and alarming thing invented than the haggis? I am of the opinion that this food was initiated to intimidate the enemy into submission.

BUTCHER BRIAN 'PERSUADES' PETA TO HAVE A GO AT HAGGIS MAKING.

Retreat was preferable to the thought of being captured and spending one's life as a prisoner to liver porridge. Our crew was ushered out the back of Leckies Butchery into a large, pristine, white room. At one end were great, steaming hunks of meat being lifted out of the boilers with a pitchfork to be placed in white plastic buckets. Off to the right was the smoking shed and in the centre sat the operating table surrounded by macabre hams and black puddings hanging from the ceiling. We were introduced to master of ceremonies — butcher Brian, a stocky, smiling man with strong arms impressively imprinted with a pandemonium of tattoos. He and all the other butchers wore blue shirts of the colour and texture of the overalls worn all over France by workers. Over this was worn a white apron covered by a blue plastic one, the whole story being topped off with white cap and white gumboots.

'Peta, I think you had better put on an apron and a cap,' suggested Chris.

'I'm not wearing that silly hat. It took me half an hour to get my hair looking the artful wreck it is,' I replied daintily.

'I'm awfully afraid you're going to have to wear it. You can't be seen handling meat inappropriately adorned,' he smiled politely.

I gulped. 'I have to touch it?' (Said the actress to the bishop).

'You have to touch it and probably worse.'

Sniggers emanated from other members of the crew, thanking God for making them technicians and not presenters.

The lamb, beef, liver and heart that had been gently boiled went into a huge mincer with mammoth onions to be beaten into submission, thence to be mixed with cooking juices, SECRET spices, salt, pepper and oatmeal. So far everybody was coping with the strong smell of flesh. Next, a gaggle of sheep's stomachs were flung by Brian on to the table. He smiled. I blanched. I closed my eyes, thought of England and began trimming the bits off these very attractive, grey-pink parts of the anatomy, turning them inside out to be stuffed. Words cannot convey the feel or aroma of these organs. All the other butchers were smiling sympathetically, and Brian assured me that the stomachs imbue the haggis with their flavour. They were stuffed with the haggis mixture by a computerised vacuum filler and tied at the end with a thick piece of string, then poached in the same cooking liquid in which the raw ingredients had been cooked. Haggis reminds me of the famous wild hare recipe: marinate for two hours in red wine, discard hare and drink wine.

Jim Leckie is a gentle, humorous man who has a definite belief system behind his business. He is the third generation of his family running this shop near the seaside at St Clair and has a personal commitment to tradition and quality of life, not only for himself but also for his staff. He is adamant about the importance of doing things the natural way without added flavour or preservatives and about imparting this knowledge to everyone who works with him. He wouldn't let so-called progress within a dozen miles (19 kilo-metres) of his shop.

'It's really good for staff to be participating in something they've made from scratch. We have fun here and pride in our work — there's no point in working if it's a slog and doesn't mean anything to you. All our products, from smoked lamb or bacon to black and white puddings, are made the old, traditional way.'

Speaking of smoking, Chris thought it would be a really good idea to shoot a sequence in the smoke house. The theory was that I would open the door to show the meat smoking and do a little ditty to camera about said process. Wood shavings from the local furniture shop in the form of beech, kauri, mahogany and willow (nothing tanalised obviously) were lit in a big pot in the tarry black metal vault that is the smoke house. Fine. You wish. Camera rolling, presenter ready in silly hat, butcher opens door to reveal tornado of black ash and smoke, cameraman experiences temporary blindness, presenter gasps asthmatically and weeps said ditty to barely visible camera, all others present vacate premises. For some inexplicable reason, this scene was edited out of the final version. Upon recovery, Jim loaded us up with my favourite sausage, black pudding, smoked lamb hams and spicy biersticks and we moved on to do some 'pretties' around the city.

This operation involved everyone except me, who made straight for Plume in George Street to study the frippery and finery therein, in as intimate detail as is only possible for one deeply submissive to the seductiveness of cloth. Afterwards I roamed around, sometimes coming across the crew filming. I liked the city and its warm, hospitable people. They say hello to you in the street and women get into the front seat of taxis, something I wouldn't do in my wildest dreams in Auckland. The feel is like the New Zealand I knew as a child. Gentler somehow. Dunedin's a pretty, well laid-out city, centered by a rather wonderful octagon. On the hill slopes above the city, Tudor-, Jacobean- and Georgian-style houses stand next to Gothic and Arts and Crafts designs. One can feel that it has a heart, both in construction and emotion.

At five o'clock I was to join the others at the decadent Savoy in the centre of the city to, God forbid, taste the haggis. I climbed up

The Haggis Ceremony – a serious event.

the long flight of stairs to be greeted by the inimitable Bede – chef and lover of regional products. Hardly had I set foot in the place, than he had me fixed up with a Speights beer and we continued in that vein until some time the next morning. The dining-room was a huge, opulent hall from another era, with mahogany pillars and delicate stained-glass windows. One could sense the well-heeled patrons of a wealthier time dripping diamonds, sharing a lobster smothered in Sauce Américaine and sipping sweet Champagne. But what was I, humble Taste New Zealand presenter with nothing going for her but a good hairdresser and a shelf full of red dye, offered? Not lobster or Bolly, I can assure you.

With a great flourish of swords, a great spitting of words and a great snorting of whisky, I was presented with a meal for which there is absolutely no excuse. It's frankly hard to argue with the pomp and ceremony of the piping in of the haggis, whatever you may think of the taste. A procession wove through the room, consisting of the mountainous Bede ('never trust a thin chef'), Gary the piper, Matt the presenter of the haggis and various other accomplices in kilts. Bede was in full whites, the piper played bravely, and what can only be described as boiled elephant testicles were proudly laid before me on a silver platter. The piping ceased and Matt, of the flashing black eyes, elbow-length hair and a way with a kilt to make a girl pay strict attention, addressed the haggis with the famous Robbie Burns poem:

Ye powrs wha mak mankind your care
And dish them out their bill o' fare.
Auld Scotland wants nae stinking ware
That jaups in luggies.
But if ye wish her grateful prayer,
Gie her a haggis!

With a presentation that left me gasping for air, Matt recited this long poem, a portion of which is given above, easily the equivalent to the haka in its passion, violence, confrontation and fierce nationalism. If there was a pop quiz afterwards, I knew he was a man not likely to be given to foolish answers. His bearing was straight and his message passionately clear as suddenly he whipped out a silver dagger, raised it high and brought it down into the

A SURREPTITIOUS WHISKY IN AN ALREADY GOOD *CAPPUCCINO*!

haggis, splitting it open for all to partake of. He and his accomplices then congratulated themselves with a glass of Wilson's whisky. Having recovered from Matt's performance with the help of a stiff gulp, I was now expected to eat a forkful of haggis, look at the camera and smile. I did actually eat it. It wasn't so bad, but I couldn't eat it in front of the camera. I couldn't smile at the camera with a mouth full of food. We did it over and over again.

'OK, Peta, why don't we try this,' Chris suggested. 'Get the food halfway to your mouth, smile at the camera, then grab the glass of whisky and drink it.' Finally an intelligent suggestion.

'No bloody trouble smiling at the camera with a mouth full of whisky, I notice,' said the lovely John.

At the end of the shoot, kindly facilitated by Marilyn of Tourism New Zealand, Bede gave Laurence and me a bunch of mesclun, a colourful platoon of capsicums and a jar of rock salt for tomorrow's cooking lesson to be staged on the high seas. We all milled around a bit, looked at each other a bit and in a marvellous process of spontaneous combustion came to the simultaneous realisation that the evening was not yet over. Bede took control and made a phone call to a local restaurant.

'Be at The Orient at seven-thirty,' was the command.

'The Orient?' we queried.

'Yes,' said the Bede. 'You are in Dunedin, this is the Gaelic name for Edinburgh, no you are not at the Firth of Forth and, yes, we're eating Chinese. One of the best restaurants in Dunedin.'

Chris beamed. 'Sounds fine to me.'

'Choice,' said Barrie.

'I'm easy,' said Laurence.

'Yes, but what about the food?' I asked.

We arrived at The Orient on Princes Street in fine fettle, the only person not wearing a skirt being Bede, and sat down to a sumptuous banquet cooked by the owner Daniel Gin's mother. It was one of those entirely blissful evenings where one has no decisions to make and the hosts and guests understand their roles. There are no vulgar questions about the menu, no snivelling about liquid refreshment and a minimum of meaningless chit chat. We simply sat down and waited for the show to begin. To our supplies of Speights were added bottles of Cabernet Merlot, placed at intervals around our large table. Jugs of water were provided for the sake of form. Pausing only to sneer at them, we threw ourselves into the serious part of the proceedings.

With the crisp, fresh whitebait fritters that actually tasted of the little silvery darlings came the inevitable request that must occur at any table made up of Scottish and Irish descendants: 'Do we have a song among us?'

Matt placed his hands on the table, closed his black eyes and sang a Scottish ballad in his fine, gravelly voice. Loud applause led to calls for the next in line to contribute a song. The serving dishes were cleared to make way for Mrs Gin's Spicy Beef and Bok Choy. I have long loved the 'at home' tradition in France of serving all the food separately but retaining the same plate for all the courses. For example, one eats the meat dish first, then the salad and then the cheese, wiping the plate in between with chunks of *baguette*. Some people prefer not to wipe their plates at all, enjoying the mingling of juices from each successive course. And so it was with this feast, the juices from the former melting into the latter. Accompanying the beef was an entirely honourable rendition of 'Wild Mountain Thyme' from Gary the piper. As the Barbecued Duck was placed on the revolving platform in the middle of the table, he followed the song with a deeply moving poem, here reproduced in all its splendour:

> I likes cider 'cause cider makes me fart
> And when I farts I smells 'orrible
> And when I smells 'orrible people leaves me alone
> And when people leaves me alone I can drink cider.
> I likes cider 'cause cider makes me fart.

After the table thumping, thigh slapping and floor stamping had died down, I was provoked into remembering that my mother comes from Tipperary and launched into 'The Seven Deadly Sins', a song involving deception, alcohol and geranium pots. This combination is, of course, used in all Irish marital disputes. As the night folded into itself, our collective heritage mingled to become one ribald choir. The groaning board was reladen as soon as it was depleted, this time with roasted chicken accompanied by grilled salt, shitake mushrooms and greens. The Bede was raging expansively about pretentious cooking habits.

'I like *Vogue Entertaining* for stealing ideas,' said I fearlessly.

'Bloody up ya nose rubbish,' snorted Bede. 'If a recipe's name is longer than the method, I refuse to have anything to do with it.'

I told him about the special sheep with big bums we were going to look at later on in the series.

'Designer sheep — wouldn't touch them,' he said, leaning back in his chair. 'Look, I've got some real racks of lamb coming in tomorrow. Can you stay an extra day for dinner? Tender as you've ever imagined. And that brings me to another point. It's about a fish recipe in your book.'

'You've read it?' I asked.

'Memorised it.'

'I'm touched.'

'But I have to say I found this particular dish a little bland,' he ventured.

'I believe the word is subtle. I learned to cook in France where they have a horror of destroying the delicate flavour of fish with overpowering sauces,' I smiled sweetly.

'Quite right. I stand corrected, dear lady,' he said.

'It's about time, Piper, that we had a lament,' boomed the Bede later on, lifting his arms in supplication.

Gary raised himself, walked to the other side of the room and standing side on to us began retuning his bagpipes for 'Ian Lovett's Lament'. He threw his whole body and concentration into one of the most deeply powerful, disquieting sounds ever invented. The physical and emotional energy required for this instrument are considerable, and that's only counting the listeners. The pervading base note never changes while the chanter renders the slow, heart-gripping melody. I wanted it never to end. The restaurant was silent, the food untouched. I've reserved him for my funeral.

'Another one, Piper!' we all cried, to which he responded with 'Iain Ruad's Lament' and 'Rainbow'.

As is completely normal with all half-Irish people, I never fail to appreciate the beauty of a morbid song.

The nature of the liquid line-up in front of my plate was brought to my attention. It comprised green tea, Wilson's whisky, water (W.C. Fields said he never touched the stuff because of what fishes do in it), Cabernet Merlot and Speights. Look, I was only sipping it all anyway. Whenever a person offers one something in Dunedin, one can't say no — it's just simply not polite. Emboldened, I asked if I might sing an Edith Piaf song in French. They all sat up very straight with political correctness, a disease I have been immunised against. PC is a crime against nature.

'I can't stand Edith Piaf. It is the most revolting drivel that my wife imposes on me regularly,' Gary shouted.

'Go on, sing it, sing it,' said Laurence. 'Don't mind them.'

I sang 'La Vie En Rose' with all the passion and hopelessness the genre deserves as they wept into their soup and swallowed their words.

'Now why can't Piaf sing like that. Would ye like another whisky lass?'

Matt wrote a poem in my diary called 'The Scottish Blessing'.

may the best ye've ever seen
Be the worst ye'll ever see.
May a moose (mouse) nae leave yer girnal (pantry)
Wi' a teardrop in its e'e (eye).
May ye stay hale and hearty
Till yer auld enough tae dee (die).
May ye always be as happy
As I wish for ye tae be.

As good parties go, this one went. Nobody wanted to leave, but an eight am shoot awaited us at the fish shop. The boss stood up. We all stood up. A whole lot of hugging, handshaking and promises to return one day went on as Daniel stood to attention at the door. I noticed one thing that night — that the best action happens when the camera stops rolling.

first thing in the morning, Barrie greeted us with the news that he fried up the left-over haggis for his breakfast and he and his family had found it singularly delicious. With that incredulous thought in mind, we paid a visit to Fresh Freddie's Wet Fish Shop. I peered through the front window that had water running down the length of it to spy kippers, scallops, crayfish, muttonbirds (who eats those things?), snapper, Muscovy duck, fish heads, mussels, blue cod . . . you name it.

We really just wanted to take some pretties but inevitably got into a conversation with the fishmonger who took us out the back. It doesn't matter how much research you do, people never tell you the whole story on the phone. When you get there you always find hidden secrets. That was what this series was to become for all of us: discovery of the hidden gastronomic secrets of New Zealand. Out the back was one of the last fish smokers in Dunedin with — guess what — dry-smoked salmon just coming out of the murky depths for us to taste: warm, succulent and subtle.

Laurence had jacked up a freshly caught salmon for a shoot Chris wanted to do by the harbour, so off we went to the docks. Young salmon have been released by the local angler's club into Otago Harbour for the past eleven years. Because they release at a time when there is plenty of food, the salmon hang around long enough to think the place is home and so return the following year for the benefit of all.

The weather had turned and was now windy and cold. So I stood there in my gummies, freezing to death, holding a heavy salmon by its gills and attempting another 'piece to camera'. I'm not very good at them and get an attack of nerves every time I have to memorise the lines. No doubt keeping in mind the haggis-eating episode, Chris said, 'Can you remember FOUR WORDS to say to the camera?'

'I can remember FOUR LETTERS,' I said.

'Well, you can't say them. This is TVNZ,' he replied quietly with his sweet smile.

John raised his eyes heavenward, an action for which I received not a few clips in my childhood. Barrie was involved in his world of sound and silence.

'Say, "There can't be many places in the world where you can take your rod and, without paying a licence fee, reel in a salmon like this,"' said Chris.

'There can't be many places in the world where you can dip your rod . . .'

'CUT!'

'There can't be many places in the world where you can just jump in . . .'

'CUT!'

'Christ!'

We decided it was time to go hunting for the 'Jersey Benne'. When the Scottish founding settlers discovered the Otago (corruption of Māori Ōtākou) Harbour, they found the area was ideal for running sheep and growing oats, wheat and barley. The place reminded them of the Midlothian countryside they had left behind and they brought with them their food traditions: mutton pie, oats for porridge and barley for whisky. These days there's white gold grown in the paddocks also: the little 'Jersey Benne' potato. This delicacy is a small, waxy, oval potato, pale yellow on the outside and white within. It has a nutty, earthy, slightly sweet flavour so delicate that it, like crayfish, shouldn't be perverted with fancy sauces or cooking methods. It should be simply boiled or steamed and eaten with Malden sea salt, freshly ground black pepper and a suggestion of butter. We didn't happen to have a cray on hand but were later to discover a surprise substitute at Port Chalmers. Because of its high moisture and low starch, the 'Jersey Benne' doesn't keep or travel well, so it has to be eaten immediately. Nowadays, one can buy them all over New Zealand during their short season in little cardboard boxes.

In a conversation between the brilliant nineteenth century French gourmand/philosopher/musician Brillat-Savarin and a

DIGGING POTATOES HIGH ABOVE THE OTAGO HARBOUR.

philistine friend, opposing theses were argued on the value of the potato:

BRILLAT-SAVARIN: Please have some potatoes, there are plenty and *après nous le déluge*.

PHILISTINE: No thanks. I esteem the potato as a preservative against famine. I know of nothing more tasteless.

BRILLAT-SAVARIN: Gastronomic heresy! If I don't get served potatoes at every meal I make a protest for the conservation of my rights.

I feel the same way as B.S. In fact being of Irish descent, I consider it my moral obligation to eat as many as I can.

The sun had come out again as we trudged up the hill to the potato paddock at Sawyer's Bay to meet farmer Steve, a man I thought, to be reckoned with. He immediately fell into the delusion that he was the director.

'I'd just like to film these potatoes up here, Steve,' said Chris.

'Nah, you're not going to film here. You're going down that hill there,' said Steve.

'Um, well actually I would prefer to start here because of the light, the slope, the view, that sort of thing,' replied Chris patiently.

'Ya don't want New Zealand to think I'm selling rubbish. These potatoes aren't ready yet.'

INSIDE EVERY POTATO GROWER IS A TELEVISION DIRECTOR WAITING TO EMERGE.

Chris won. He almost always does in the nicest possible way. Steve was very in love with his steep, craggy, limey land and talked of his respect for the trees and native bush. People want to buy his high land for the sensational view.

'Wouldn't sell it, not even for buckets of money. The buggers will ruin my water supply. Water is everything here,' he said. 'My father only did potatoes on this land, but I've built it up into every sort of vegetable you can imagine. Big money in yams. *Big* money. Yep. Oh yeah.'

Eventually we did film the patch Steve wanted us to do. I had to dig up some spuds in my frock and boots. Steve, who works sixteen hours a day, seven days a week, exhorted me to take my sunglasses off and get my back into it.

'You look better with your glasses off, lass. Don't like a woman if I can't see the expression in her eyes.'

Then commenced a phenomenon closely aligned to

schizophrenia, wherein the interviewee develops two personalities — one off camera and one on. Off camera, Steve was funny, bossy and talkative. On camera he became wooden, literal and serious. How to get him to loosen up? We went over the questions and answers so he knew what to say without thinking (I should try that with men more often). There was a particularly hilarious story he had told me about a potato auction that I wanted him to repeat. There was another about the people who had paid a fortune for the 'Jersey Benne', then mashed them — an act of vandalism I considered terribly mad and wicked. However, Steve just froze the minute the camera was turned on. We did it again and again. Eventually, I lost it and used a method of relaxation that has never worked before but that I keep using because of a personality flaw. I grabbed my hair in my hands and screamed, 'Tell the bloody story, you fool of a man,' to which he visibly recoiled about half a metre.

'Don't do that,' he said, 'now you're acting like a woman.'

The rest of the crew were in paroxysms, falling all over the precious plants, but Steve did eventually tell me the story.

We ate a pie (extra for the tomato sauce) and a cup of tea, the preferred meal of the entire crew except me, before keeping our *rendezvous* with Maureen and George of Southern Seas Suppliers at Port Chalmers. I was there to check out their *Chlamys delicatula* (queen scallops). We all squeezed into the little office up front for a chat and to wait for their boat the *Lady Dorothy* to come in. Instant coffee was dispensed all round by the beautiful Maureen, who had very serious hair (we're talking volume and height here). I have to say I met quite a few women with serious hair on my travels for this show. Later on, I was to meet Fleur of Oliver's Lodge in Clyde whose thatch was as white as Maureen's was black. We missed a photographic study there, I think.

While I admired the quantitive coiffure, Maureen told me how to keep Steve's 'Jersey Bennes' from going green until I got back to Auckland.

'The thing that makes them deteriorate is light. If you can keep them in the dark, they'll last for ages,' she said. 'As soon as I get mine I bury them in the backyard and take them out as I need them. They keep there for a good couple of months.'

But back to the scallops. Southern Seas trawl the scallop beds that lie in deep, cold, brilliantly clear waters about ten miles (16 kilometres) beyond the harbour mouth. These scallops are special to Dunedin and I've never seen them anywhere else: small (about the size of a clam) with both psychedelic shells curved. When I saw a basket of the shells in the office, I thought they had been painted; but no, the bright orange, pink, yellow and white are as nature intended them. They are difficult to catch because they can avoid trawling nets, swimming quickly by clapping their shells together and jetting along with the force of the expelled water.

As a landlubber by nature I was extremely relieved that we weren't actually going to hit the high seas physically but film my interview and cooking lesson with Captain Steve in dry dock, as it were. Fortunately, I was wrapped in something very fisherpersony in the form of a thickly ribbed, deep-purple sweater from Nom D, which achieved the extraordinary feat of having sleeves almost the same length as my body. Needless to say, being from Dunedin where they feel the cold only when icicles start forming on their Speights,

CAPTAIN STEVE, READY TO DEVOUR THE SCALLOPS COOKED IN CREAM AND WHISKY.

Steve was in a T-shirt. John was turning around in circles in the little cabin muttering such things as 'ya smell of fish ya big brute' to no one in particular. Laurence had come equipped to the gills with ingredients and cooking utensils.

The following is equipment required to cook a meal in a square foot of space for a television show:

1. Portable gas burner.

2. Weight loss programme.

3. Excellent sense of balance and timing.

4. Photographic memory.

5. Fire extinguisher.

6. Ability to take executive decisions around whisky bottles.

The blue-eyed (are all fishermen blue-eyed?), fair-haired Steve never really managed to get the startled look off his face, but he did like what I did with his scallops. We had decided that the beasties would be cooked in cream, dill, garlic and flambéd with whisky. Laurence showed me how to flambé without losing my fringe. All set, camera rolling. Steve and I chatted while I made the dish, then the flambé moment arrived.

'And now I'm just going to chuck this whisky in here A-N-D . . . nothing.' Unmistakable non-igniting of flame. Distinct lack of fire. Laurence frantically doing clever imitation of the sign language person on TV. Eventually it worked and I thanked Laurence for his patience and good inter-personal skills which was when he confided in me his two big rules in life:

'As far as getting on with women goes,' he said, 'there are only two simple rules. Rule number one is the woman is always right. Rule number two is if you don't think she's right refer to rule number one.' I knew we would get along. He's a worrier, so I told him about my two rules:

1. Don't sweat the small stuff.

2. It's all small stuff.

THE CREW ARE ALWAYS READY TO EAT THE PROPS. (LEFT IS JOHN, THE LOCAL CAMERAMAN.)

By then we had cooked enough queen scallops to feed the whole New Zealand army. In an oft-to-be-repeated gesture of solidarity, the crew fell on the food. Even then there was a lot left over so we went outside to the deck and fed all the other fishermen hanging around waiting to unload the boat of its tons of scallops. They were impressed and asked for the recipe, inscribed below.

TVNZ QUEEN SCALLOPS

ONE BIG HANDFUL PER PERSON OF SCALLOPS IN THEIR SHELLS, CLEANED
LOTS OF CHOPPED GARLIC
BUNCH OF CHOPPED FRESH DILL
SMALL BOTTLE OF CREAM
FRESHLY GROUND PEPPER
WHISKY

Heat a deep, heavy-based pan over high heat then put in scallops. Cover and cook on high heat till they are just open, shaking occasionally. Remove lid and add chopped garlic, dill, cream and pepper. Toss for a minute to heat the sauce, then throw in a good tipple of whisky, tipping the pan a little to ensure a very hot surface for the whisky to catch flame. When fire is extinguished eat these sweet, tender little scallops with some steamed Jersey Bennes and a blue-eyed fisherman.

Note: When cooking this meal, always invite Peta around to share it, otherwise it will stick in your throat and taste salty from your lonely tears.

LAKE ELLESMERE.

christchurch

U *n dessert sans fromage est une belle a qui il manque un oeil* — a dessert without cheese is a beautiful woman with an eye missing

BRILLAT-SAVARIN

We'd just settled down with the women's magazines, trying to make sense of such headlines as I SLEPT WITH MY MOTHER'S PRIMARY SCHOOL TEACHER'S SON'S ADOPTED DAUGHTER and DISTRAUGHT MOTHER DROWNS ALIEN SEXTUPLETS BEFORE HUSBAND GETS HOME FOR SUPPER. How any normal person can possibly fly in a plane or work out at a gym without the women's mags is beyond the realms of human understanding. Planes and gyms are intoxicatingly boring normally, but not this one. The plane hadn't even taken off, we hadn't even realised that it was one of those aberrant flights that DOESN'T SERVE ALCOHOL, when Laurence noticed they were putting in more fuel.

'Um,' he said, 'you never fuel a plane full of passengers. Something's going on.'

'Ladies and gentlemen, please fasten your safety belts,' said the captain.

'They're fuelling and we have to fasten our safety belts? This isn't right,' said Laurence.

'Did you know that Princess Di can't get a date because of cellulite on her thighs?' I asked, reading one of the magazine articles.

'For God's sake,' said Chris.

'Ladies and gentlemen,' announced the pilot, 'there will be a delay on take-off due to an earthquake that has just occurred in Christchurch.'

We all burst into laughter, and I thought, 'What a wonderful sense of humour Dunedin people have and where's my whisky?'

'We are taking on more fuel in case we can't land at Christchurch Airport,' continued the captain. Where we might end up was anyone's guess. Preferred destinations that came to mind were Bolivia, the South of France and Palm Springs.

Unfortunately, none of those things happened and we spent the evening haggling over who would get the honeymoon suite at the motel in Christchurch. Finally, we let Laurence have it and it turned out the water-bed leaked and the spa bath didn't work. In the morning the first shoot was outside the Six Chairs Missing Café, where I almost got six hairs and a nose missing when a tram went past. We were met by our Christchurch cameraman Graham and sound man Don. My sidewalk table had been placed too close to the tracks as I screamed to the camera on the other side of the road, 'Anyone who hasn't been to Christchurch for a year or two is going to be astonished with what's been going on here.' I'll say. Around the corner in the red-light district, Chris pointed out signs that said GIRLS GIRLS GIRLS and just below, MAKE YOUR OWN SANDWICH. We thought and thought what that might have meant.

I went for a little ride on one of the antique trams and took keen note of the instructions on the wall. 'Important: expectorating within the car is prohibited. Any person so offending will be ejected and prosecuted.' It seemed to me there was a lot of voiding going on in there. It reminded me of the stupid standard one joke about a man who was about to meet the Queen and, out of nervousness, farted.

'How dare you fart before the Queen,' said Prince Philip.

'I'm terribly sorry, I didn't know it was her turn,' the man gasped.

These trams are museum pieces, not replicas. They were made in the late 1800s and early 1900s and saw many years' service, sometimes behind horses. They were thrown away, then found and lovingly restored. Now five of them grace the central-city tourist circuit, clanking past Korean, Japanese, Mongolian and French restaurants. While the rest of the crew did some pretties, I made for

PHILOMENA SELLING HOT GAELIC BREAD AT THE CHRISTCHURCH ARTS CENTRE MARKET.

that mausoleum of destruction, that mansion of subversion, that monument to glitz: the casino (derived from an Italian word meaning brothel). I couldn't even garner up enough interest to spend one dollar, but wandered around transfixed by the faces of the middle-aged punters. People are suggesting that women are the future problem gamblers of New Zealand because the casino becomes a social outing. You can get dressed up, you can meet men (I'm only repeating what I heard) and you can have an endorphin rush not commonly seen outside the gym. Personally, I prefer *la gourmandise*.

Mid-morning saw us trying to pry Joe Graham out from under

the table at his bakehouse in Addington. Canterbury was once considered to be the granary of New Zealand. The farmer who didn't grow wheat ran sheep, so it wasn't surprising that the local diet seemed to be dominated by bread and mutton. Canterbury is still the bread basket and the recent big discovery is Irish bread: Soda Bannocks, Barmbracks, Guinness Loaves, Potato Bread and more. The Addington bakehouse is small considering its huge output. Just a few years ago after Joe was made redundant from Telecom, he and his wife (possessed of the most flamboyant name, Philomena) went to Ireland and got the idea of starting up a little bread-making business as a hobby. I always look on strangely named people with sympathy, remembering what I went through at the suburban gulag called school, at the hands of five-year-old sadists called primers. They made me sit on the boys' seats because I had a boy's name. Don't make me talk about it because I'll cry. Phil says her mother gave her that name so she wouldn't forget it.

For twenty years, since immigrating to New Zealand, they had dreamed of eating the real Irish bread with which they had grown up, so they garnered the old recipes and brought them back to Christchurch. In County Antrim, Joe learned the art of baking traditional Gaelic bread, and he even brought back with him samples of the local flour so it could be specially milled for him here. The 'hobby' lasted about six months, turning into an affair that sees Joe working an average twelve hours a day in a business with which he can barely keep up. Which brings me to why we are dragging him out from under the table. Not only is he shy but he would much rather be at home asleep than pratting around in front of a camera, dying of embarrassment every time I ask him a question. Unlike his youngest son who is a natural. A gangster, his mother calls him: open, charming, and totally fearless in the face of a television crew.

'So, Joe,' I said. 'Tell me about this Irish bread.'

'Do I *have* to now?'

The reticence was beguiling and I was determined to get my hands on one of those potato breads he was making. More potatoes — there is a God after all.

'Can I bribe you with some of that Guinness you're so recklessly pouring into your mixture?' I asked.

'Can't stand Guinness.'

'Whisky?'

'Never touch the stuff.'

'You're not Irish and don't lie to your mother.'

He burst out laughing and we proceeded with the interview. Joe refused to give me any recipes for his bread, but I did notice that wholemeal flour, soda flour, raw sugar, baking soda and buttermilk went into the Guinness Bread along with a glass, per loaf, of the delicious black liquid. In one of my Irish cookbooks at home, I found a recipe for Soda Bread.

Bread making like pastry making is one of those things that, with practice, suddenly makes sense one day. It can't really be taught. One keeps doing it with a light, quick touch until it works, and then, like riding a bike, one never forgets. I have found that drinking Guinness while I work is the secret to truly memorable bread making. Soda Bread is particularly easy as you don't have to fuss around with esoteric, capricious things like yeast. Bicarbonate of soda and kneading are the two things that influence the texture of the bread. Too much soda will discolour and spoil the taste, and too much kneading with too dry a dough will produce a heavy loaf. You can substitute some of the sour milk with sour cream, buttermilk or whey to enrich it.

IRISH SODA BREAD

620 g/4 cups WHITE FLOUR
140 g/1 cup WHOLEMEAL FLOUR
55 g/½ cup OATMEAL
2 tsp BICARBONATE OF SODA
1 tsp SALT
470-720 ml/2-3 cups SOUR MILK

Mix dry ingredients very well in a large bowl. Pour in enough of the milk so that the dough is wet enough to knead easily. Turn out on to a floured bench and knead lightly for a few minutes. Form into a round, place on a greased oven tray and mark with a cross. Bake in a fairly hot oven (200°C) for about half an hour.

While I was hanging around waiting for the camera and sound to set up, I read the tea-towels pinned to the wall:

'May you be in heaven half an hour before the devil knows you're dead.'

'The older the fiddle the sweeter the tune' — similar to the French expression *'les meilleur daubes sont faites dans les plus anciennes marmites'* (the best stews are made in the oldest pots).

'What butter and whiskey will not cure, there's no cure for.'

'You'll never plough a field by turning it over in your mind.'

Not only do Joe and Phil have a shop in Merivale to sell their breads but they also tend a stall at the Art Centre Market. A day without Philomena would be like an eclipse. We fell upon each other immediately, exchanging strict-mother stories. A real Irish beauty from Holywood in County Down with blue eyes, red hair and rosy cheeks, she filled up the screen like a sunburst. Phil is the sort of person you want to keep talking to for ever, and I can see all her customers feel the same way. They can't bear not to be with her, and when they do move on she smiles and sparkles,

'You have a nice day, do you hear me now?'

'Phil,' I asked, 'how long does this bread last?'

'Oh, sure it depends how fast you eat it.'

We both collapsed into gales of laughter. Chris stood by patiently.

'How many Irishmen does it take to tile a floor?' I asked.

'Glory be to God, I wouldn't know,' she replied. 'How many?'

'It depends on how thinly you slice them.'

Screams of laughter. The older son stood nearby, rigid with shyness and the fear that I and the camera would address him. His father's son.

'How did you manage with Joe?' Phil asked.

'He was a bit shy but fine in the end,' I replied.

'God love him. Why didn't you give him a vodka, Peta?'

'So that's the secret! I'm a Guinness person myself, how about you?'

'Oh, me, too,' she replied. 'I love stout, and do you know what? I always find the second and third ones taste best.'

Philomena wrote a poem in my diary:

bannocks and Barmbracks to name but a few,
    These are the breads we have for you.
All healthy and tasty, some spiced with good luck,
They're ready and waiting at our wee shop.
Go on spoil yourself — come down for a treat,
Try Graham's Gaelic Bread at 1 Twigger Street.

THE BARRY'S BAY CHEESE FACTORY.

We didn't have to travel far to find some good cheese at one of the first areas in New Zealand to export cheese; in fact, dairy farming had got underway round about the time when Akaroa was still a French settlement. It is the southernmost French settlement in the world, still bearing French street names and architecture, and the oldest town in the South Island. In 1938 the captain of a French whaling ship negotiated with a local Māori chief to buy Banks Peninsula. He returned to France to get his sixty-three immigrants, but by the time he got back to New Zealand in 1840, British sovereignty had been established. Having made the long journey, the settlers decided to stay and made their home at Akaroa.

All cheese making was carried out by the early settlers on their farms using primitive equipment like chessets (cheese moulds) and presses brought with them from England and Scotland. Moulds and vats were wooden, and presses were set up between tree stumps, with stones on levers to press the cheese. The clean, fertile pastures of the Peninsula produce some of the finest milk around. At Barry's Bay Cheese, we once again met people, like Jim Leckie in Dunedin, who are committed to using only natural ingredients and adhering to traditional methods. Don and Jeanette Walker make a range of semi-soft and hard cheeses, like rinded Cheddars, Havarti, Maasdam, Edam and Canterbury red among others, in their strictly hygienic factory, where yet again I got to pretend I was a brain surgeon in a silly hat and white coat. I bought an eight-year-old rinded Cheddar wrapped in muslin and wax, and I took it to every dinner I went to once I got back home to Auckland, like a poodle. It met with great approval and admiration.

'**n**o! You're not interviewing me,' shouted Lyn of Tree Crop Farm. 'No, I told the man you can do what you like but I'm not getting in front of the camera.'

'But we've come here to interview you,' pleaded Chris.

'No.'

'But the famous *cappuccino-lattes*?'

'Peta can make them.'

Chris and I looked at each other. As the saying goes, once the improbable has been ruled out, the solution must lie in the realm of the impossible. Right. No interview. I knew what that meant. It meant I would have to say more than four words to the camera. Finally, after tactful and polite negotiation on the parts of Chris and Laurence (the English do have that tendency), Lyn agreed to be filmed making the famous *cappuccino-lattes* but on condition that only her hands showed. Laurence had discovered Tree Crop Farm while on holiday and thought it would be a spicy story.

Lyn's home has been opened up to the public for bed and breakfast and also afternoon teas. The most obvious thing about her extended house in the countryside on Rue Grehan at Akaroa was the sayings written in chalk all over the walls:

'Grow your own dope — plant a man.'

'Cooking is like a love affair — enter with abandon or not at all.'

'A gentleman is a man who can play the piano accordion — and doesn't.'

'Hell hath no fury like the lawyer of a woman scorned.'

'Fashion is a form of slavery so intolerable that we have to change it every six months.'

My question is can too much advice be fatal to humans? These sayings were not only all over the walls but all over the surrounding hills, behind rose bushes and on walks around the property.

Some of the furniture, walls and floors had been painted gold, a touch I approved of in this unrepentantly riotous decor. Photographs, old furniture, large open windows, huge baskets of walnuts, extravagant vases of flowers, blue glasses and pottery, jasmine wrapped around the wash basin and cistern in the bathrooms. All this led out on to an open lounge/large porch that looked out on to the hills now covered in drizzling rain. All around this area was a rolled-up marine-blue canvas that could be lowered in the winter. This heavenly room was full of sofas covered in sheepskin rugs and skins, chirping birds, a Shetland pony, rough manuka furniture and low tables covered in flowers, giant nut-crackers and books.

'No! You can't film the pony. You can film it walking by but you can't film it in the house,' ordered Lyn. Right.

Lyn, a lady who doesn't mince words, has invented her own way of making a *cappuccino* that bears little relationship to the classic Italian method involving warm frothy milk being poured gently into a cup of espresso. Her coffee making has become a ritual in itself as is everything she does in this house. The CD is playing 'Ave Mundi Luminar' by Rodrigo Leão and the Vox Ensemble, a passionate combination of Portuguese and classical music. All is beauty and calm as the white-braided Lyn sets to her task with a domestic Ariette machine. She presents the separate parts of her *cappuccino-latte* made from fresh coffee beans to the customer on a wooden tray — a large warmed mug full of piping hot, frothy, trim milk, a small mug full of espresso with a perfect crema on top, a silver bowl of raw sugar and a tiny mahogany box of freshly grated nutmeg.

One pours as much of the coffee as one wishes into the mug of milk, then sprinkles over the nutmeg. Accompanying the coffee were slices of Russian cake, a delicious concoction resembling *Pan Forte*. Lyn was adamant about how people really want to drink a *cappuccino*.

'People like lots of milk. They don't like strong coffee or inferior quality coffee,' she said. 'As the espresso is in a separate mug, the client can see for themselves the high quality of the beans.'

I wanted to say I liked strong coffee with little milk, but I was too scared.

This business necessitated a long piece to camera, and because I was having such a good time playing with the coffee, I wasn't as nervous as usual. In fact, the fear of the camera and the embarrassment of presenting to all these people was receding, despite the misunderstandings. Having zero experience and working with very experienced people, there were lots of expressions I didn't understand. It took me a long time to figure out when I could start speaking once the camera was rolling. There were many times where we all just stood silently looking at one another. Words for GO include the following:

Frame

Rolling

You're on

I'm ready

Mumble

Action

Silence (telepathic communication)

Eye movements resembling the ones the nuns gave me at school

I have to mention here as a digression, my friend Tanah's cheat *cappuccino*. If you can't get down to Akaroa and can't possibly make it to your local canteen, this is the solution:

> **M**ake coffee in plunger from freshly ground beans. Bring a whole lot of milk to the boil. Pour coffee into a jug to keep it warm. Rinse plunger and pour in hot milk. Froth milk by pushing plunger up and down rapidly. Put coffee in warmed cups, pour frothy milk on top and grate some nutmeg over it.
>
> Go back to bed.

because it was raining and because I was wearing a long skirt and a natty arrangement of green silk and lace, Chris just knew it was the right time to have me go for a walk on Tree Crop Farm and climb over some fences. When I saw the edited version of this sequence I screamed, 'No more kneecaps!' I found out that they tell me they've stopped filming, then they just continue and put those bits in to entertain themselves.

There are signed tracks all over the farm that clients enjoy as a part of their stay. 'Pain is inevitable, misery is optional' is scrawled on a seat overlooking the most idyllic scene of bubbling brook and lupin-lined walkway. That was another thing likable about the South Island along with the people: happy lupins everywhere in every delightful colour. I personally never notice gardens because my mouth is always full (figure that one out) but lupins are so big and radiant I can't avoid seeing them.

Lodging at the farm comes in the form of three wooden huts near the main house. One has an electric shower, but guests prefer the *au naturel* ones with no electricity, pot-bellied stoves and starlight baths. Our favourite that we filmed was green and gold with nothing in it but a double bed, candles and flowers. Covered in roses, it looked out on to a little stream and waterfall. Nearby, hidden by lupins, roses and jasmine sat a gold bathtub surrounded by candles and lit by a fire underneath. We foolishly attempted to film it.

'No. No!' came the order from the kitchen window. 'Now, I've told you about this already. You're not shooting the bathtubs in daylight. It's a non-event. Has to be done at night with the candles and darkness and everything. By God, you TV people are all the same — got to watch you like a hawk!'

'OK,' said Chris, 'I think we've got enough anyway.'

By that time we loved the place so much we didn't want to leave, Lyn was chilling out and Laurence had taken it upon himself to read every saying on the walls.

'If you don't leave you will have to light up the bathtubs — I've got guests tonight,' said Lyn.

'OK, we're off.'

We were staying at a motel right on the harbour and Lyn had suggested we eat at C'est La Vie restaurant if we could get in. My room was on ground level and I sat four metres from the water, listening to the waves and inhaling the pungent smell of seaweed. The rain had stopped, everything felt fresh, and the mist hung around the hills. Ducks waddled past on the grass whispering to each other as I girded my loins for a gastronomic blowout.

We arrived at C'est La Vie starving to death with hope in our hearts and wine in our arms. Fortunately, we didn't have to indulge in hypoglycaemic attacks all over the steps because the menu was actually written on blackboards either side of the front steps leading into the tiny restaurant. We had to make up our minds there and then what we wished to eat. We were seated in a small room that catered for just twenty and the feeling of being in someone's dining-room was accentuated by the traditional decor of embroidered tablecloths, candles in wine bottles and medieval-style chairs. The food was also traditional in the sense that it was 'unfashionable' by current standards, but as soon as it was put in front of you, you devoured it as if you hadn't eaten for a year. My body, which has now been educated to eat healthily, saw prawns in cream sauce, potatoes cooked in cream and garlic, rack of lamb with hollandaise sauce, and every pathetic cholesterol-starved cell opened its little arms and begged on its little knees for more. Gentle reader, the lamb went in, the deep-fried pear-shaped potatoes went in and the buttered beans went in.

Our hostess was Magdalena, a fey-like, gentle, softly spoken woman from Cologne, and her husband Charlie manned the ovens. In a habit I learned from ten years of living in Paris, I went straight into the kitchen after dinner to thank the chef and chat with him. This is something that is rarely done here but French restaurant kitchens are always full of visitors talking about food. Our meal was served in the European way where no matter what you had ordered, everyone got a mixed salad to start. The mains arrived on large platters with silver spoons to serve ourselves, and we retained the same knives and forks throughout the meal. The crew were ecstatic. They thought they had died and gone to heaven. It was one of the best meals I ate in the whole series.

at some point in each segment I would be filmed driving one of our red rental cars with a big AVIS sign stuck on to the number plate. It usually involved driving the car down the road or into a location or some such thing. Simple. So, why was I in a gully with a huge drainpipe in synthesis with my back wheel? At the top of the hill the crew drooped their shoulders.

'Can't even drive a car down a hill and turn around again.'

'So she is blonde under all that red.'

'Yep. I could see that coming.'

I imagined they said these things, but what they really did was walk down the hill smiling wordlessly. In an instant replay of boy-scout days, they threw themselves into the task of relieving the shiny red car of its attachment to the rocks and mud. As one man they quietly united. It was deeply moving. There is a use for men after all, I thought, aside from planting them. They put logs nicked from a nearby property under the wheel, jacked it up, and *voilà*, a liberated wheel. In case anyone from Avis is reading this, there was no damage done to the car, OK?

'Where else would you like me to drive?' I asked Chris brightly.

'Nowhere! I'm going to find a red wig,' he replied.

'Just take hers off and give it a shake,' suggested Graham, 'No one will know.'

Eventually, we made it to Alan and Celia Hay's farm in Pigeon Bay to check out the big-bottomed sheep, the Inveralloch lamb, bred from a Coopworth/texel cross and a South Suffolk ram. Fast growing and meaty, this specialist sheep is never drenched and never dipped.

Any that require treatment go back into the main mob, so the meat from the select flock is chemical-free and used almost exclusively in Celia's restaurant in Christchurch: Hay's Café & Wine Bar. Celia specialises in lamb dishes in her new prize-winning restaurant, for example, Roast Lamb, Lamb Burger, Lamb *Souvlaki* and Thai Lamb Salad. The Hays also have a delicatessen, kitchenware shop and cooking school. On top of all that, they care for the baby and grow a beautiful garden.

'Our lamb is quite special,' said Celia. 'We live by the sea and I'm sure the fresh air, natural salt and the lack of drenches helps the flavour and texture. The meat is killed at a local abattoir, boned out by our butcher, then the chefs work over the meat removing all unnecessary sinew. The lamb is marinated in olive oil before cooking.'

Taking with us a couple of the loins, we rushed to be on time for our ten o'clock shoot with chef Peter Thornley at French Farm restaurant at French Farm Bay. What a joke. He was still in bed and didn't turn up till eleven. We wandered around outside the large, two-storeyed, ochre house, bumping into staff looking the worse for wear after what had apparently been a humdinger of a wedding the night before. I asked for a coffee to try to delude myself that I hadn't eaten thirty-seven million calories last evening and it was served to me on a tray with all the trimmings. Such nice people. So easy to sit under the soft-hued, buttercup-coloured roses, scribbling away in my little notebook. 'Be quiet,' the crew now say to one another, 'she's writing. Don't say anything you don't want the whole country to know. Look what she did to those people in France.' I could have been back in France: off to my left were vineyards and everywhere were flowers, lushness, groves, verdure. I spied the sous-chef picking handfuls of herbs from the garden.

Screech of brakes — Peter and Jane had arrived. I sneaked into the kitchen to say hello to a tall, dark, handsome (I swear) man with bloodshot eyes and a brave smile. He was prepping the botanical orgy we would later film

'BE QUIET,' THE CREW SAY TO ONE ANOTHER, 'SHE'S WRITING!'

and subsequently fall upon: Wood-Roasted Peppers. Four times Peter has been crowned Singapore's chef of the year, and he's worked all over the world bringing light and happiness to many kitchens. He was relaxed and funny and we got to talking about the challenge of working to a camera.

'I can see you're going to be an easy person to interview,' I said gratefully.

'There's a secret. When I first did a cooking show in Wellington, I was absolutely hopeless. Wooden would be an understatement and there was no way I could smile,' he replied.

'I'm so glad you shared that with me. How did you get over it?'

'The cameraman stuck a *Playboy* centrefold on the tripod just below the lens, so every time I looked up I grinned. Worked wonders.'

'Oh, I see, so all I have to do is pretend the cameraman is naked?'

'Peta, we don't want you fainting — we only want a smile.'

PICINC AT FRENCH FARM.

The previous day, Peter had washed the red peppers, halved, emptied and salted them and left them to sit for twenty-four hours to remove the liquid. Now he was washing the salt off and rubbing the peppers in olive oil and herbs like thyme and rosemary, ready to be roasted. Next, a tray was filled with a heady mixture of manuka and kanuka shavings, bay leaves, thyme sprigs, star anise and cinnamon sticks, which Peter covered with tin foil, slashing an opening in the top. For the lamb loins we had brought him, Peter ground up an exotic pastiche of Asian spices that tasted more Moroccan to me. Just the smell of them reminded me of home-made *Harissa*, *Tagines* and *Couscous* and sent me into a delicious reverie of many good meals had with Arab friends in France. Peter even keeps his seasoning in a two-hundred-year-old, carved-wood, North-

African spice box. This man is no slouch. He speaks rapid-fire, inundates you with ideas and jokes ceaselessly. In his 'spare time' he looks after the gardens, makes balsamic vinegar and concocts infusions for the olive oil he imports from Italy. He doesn't see why the public should pay a fortune for imported flavoured oils, so he has developed a way of making his own, which he uses himself in the kitchen and also sells — coriander oil, mandarin oil, herb oil, chilli oil and others.

Because the oven has to be at such a high temperature to smoke the peppers, Peter usually warns everyone to vacate the premises. The tray of wood shavings is placed on the lower shelf of the oven and the tray of peppers on the upper. Ten minutes later you open the oven door, quickly grab the peppers and wood shavings, dump them on the bench and run. The kitchen has by now filled with black smoke and anyone who is foolish enough to still be there (like cameramen, sound men, directors and presenters) weep and splutter on the floor. Slight exaggeration, but you get the picture.

The lamb loins, which had been brushed with coriander and mandarin oils then spread with the spice mixture, were thrown on to a searing hot *teppanyaki* grill.

'Six solid inches (150 millimetres) of stainless steel,' grinned Peter. 'You can cook a lot of food very fast on this thing.'

Once sealed on both sides, the loins were placed in a hot oven to finish. Chris and Laurence had arranged a picnic down the road with all the goodies we had collected in Christchurch. The lamb and peppers couldn't be served the way they normally are in the restaurant, so a sandwich was invented on the spot involving sliced lamb, peppers and 'Cos' lettuce leaves instead of bread.

'I CAN SEE YOU'RE GOING TO BE AN EASY PERSON TO INTERVIEW,' SAID PETA TO PETER.

Our final afternoon in Akaroa saw Peter and me enjoying our picnic in the cold under a tree by the water, surrounded by Irish breads, Barry's Bay cheeses, white wine and hungry crew. Vinaigrette was poured over the sandwich and we dived in. Have you ever tried eating a huge, precarious bunch of food without ruining your lipstick? How come in movies the woman never gets messed up and never spills the sauce on her dress and always looks graceful and never falls over laughing? Hey! It's a tough job, but someone has to do it.

PETER THORNLEY'S MARINATED LAMB

2 STAR ANISE

4 CLOVES

1/4 CINNAMON STICK

2 cm PIECE OF FRESH GINGER

2 CLOVES OF GARLIC

2 tbsp CHINESE ROCK SUGAR

1 tsp CORIANDER SEEDS

1/2 tsp PEPPERCORNS

1/2 tsp ROCK SALT

1/4 tsp FRESHLY GRATED NUTMEG

4 CARDAMOMS

4 TRIMMED LAMB LOINS

MANDARIN-INFUSED OLIVE OIL

CORIANDER-INFUSED OLIVE OIL

Grind all the spices and mix to a paste with a little oil. Coat the loins in the infused oils, then the spice mixture. Let them rest in the fridge for eight hours under a weight. Sear both sides in a very hot oven-proof fry-pan, then place in a very hot oven for about three minutes, so that they are still pink in the middle. Remove from oven and cool.

A simplified way for the innocent civilian at home to smoke peppers is to put the manuka mixture in a big, heavy-based pot or saucepan, get it smoking over a very high heat, then place a sieve full of prepared peppers over it. Cover tightly with the lid and release after ten minutes. When I got home, I tried the pepper recipe to great acclaim, if I may say so, but I used the oven method. Checking that the insurance on the house had been paid, I fearlessly put the wood shavings in the oven and within four minutes they were on fire. The trick is to put lots of shavings in and also it is essential to cover them with tin foil slashed in the middle. Also most domestic ovens will never reach the temperature of a professional one, so I found the peppers benefited from being left in the oven with the shavings for another five minutes with the oven turned off.

To make an inspired lunch on a hot summer's day, simply make a bed of mixed salad greens on four dinner plates. On top of that place some roasted peppers and a natty arrangement of cold, sliced lamb. Pour over a vinaigrette made from two parts olive oil, one part balsamic vinegar, roasted sesame seeds, a little soy sauce and Dijon mustard. In side dishes you can serve preserved lemon slices, toasted sesame seeds and sea salt to sprinkle at will. Remove lipstick and eat.

CHAMPAGNE POOLS AT WAI-O-TAPU.

CHAPTER THREE

rotorua

kia hora te marino, kia whakapapa pounamu te moana, kia tere te kārohirohi i mua i tōu huarahi, āianei ā ake tonu atu — may the calm be widespread, may the sea glisten like greenstone, and may the shimmer of sunlight ever cross your pathway in life, now and always

In between the Christchurch shoot and this one, I had discovered another facet of my job: voice-overs. You stand all alone in a soundproofed room watching little numbers turning over on the screen and getting blasts of incredibly loud music because the technician forgot to turn it down. This was the first time I had seen an edited segment, and I kept missing my cues because my mouth was open in horror and/or fascination at what I was seeing. Don't waste $120 an hour on a shrink. If you want to know yourself as others see you, get a job with television. Your tone of voice, body language and every lie you ever told your mother are all there in unmistakable, justly feared detail with a few pounds added on by the camera.

Chris and Laurence were already down in Rotorua, birthplace of my father and his family, doing 'reccies'. I emerged from the TVNZ van at Whakarewarewa village with cameraman Dave and sound man John the following day, raring to go. Our first shoot was inside the cool whare, where a concert party was performing to a full house of tourists. It was wonderful to listen to those beautiful waiata I hadn't heard for so long. How boring our culture would be without the Māori. I sat on the floor in bare feet, closed my eyes and listened to the mellifluous harmonies. The leader of the group was explaining about Māoritanga in that articulate, eloquent way all innate orators have.

The day continued to heat up as we trailed all our equipment around to the hot pools in the village, where some women were boiling sweet corn in the pool to sell to the tourists. A man offered me a very overcooked morsel — Māori have never heard of minimalism in terms of cooking. The idea of this shoot was to show the way in which thermal energy is used for cooking. Next to the pools were steam boxes to facilitate ngāwhā (steam) cooking, and this was when I met the gracious, sparkling Emily Schuster who showed me how it was done. The food doesn't actually go in the water — it sits on a shelf in the oven and gets steamed. She had already put down corned beef, a highly under-rated food in my opinion, as is boiled lamb and chicken. Call me old-fashioned but there is something to be said for a chook simply boiled with herbs and a few vegetables for taste, then served covered in a smooth béchamel sauce enriched with nutmeg and egg yolks. And what about the French *Gigot de Sept Heures*? — Seven-Hour Lamb in which a leg of lamb (mutton would be even better) is roasted for seven hours in a very slow oven. I made this once when I was chef on a barge in the Upper Loire and when it was cooked one could eat it with a spoon.

BOILED CHICKEN WITH BECHAMEL SAUCE

FOR THE STUFFING:

35 g FRESH BREADCRUMBS

12 ml MILK

200 g GROUND HAM OR BACON

2 CLOVES OF GARLIC, CHOPPED

2 tbsp FRESH SAGE OR TARRAGON, CHOPPED

CHICKEN LIVER AND HEART, CHOPPED

1 EGG, BEATEN

SALT AND FRESHLY GROUND PEPPER

TRUSSING NEEDLE AND STRING

1 LARGE CHICKEN

500 g SMALL TURNIPS, PEELED

1 kg LEEKS, WELL WASHED, THE GREEN PART TRIMMED OFF

750 g CARROTS, PEELED

1 STALK OF CELERY

SALT AND BLACK PEPPERCORNS

BOUQUET GARNI (PARSLEY, THYME AND BAY LEAF TIED UP IN MUSLIN)

1 ONION, PEELED AND STUDDED WITH 3 CLOVES

To make the stuffing, soak the breadcrumbs in the milk and squeeze dry. Add the other ingredients, mix well and stuff and truss the bird. Place the chicken in a large pot with all the other ingredients, cover with water, cover and simmer for an hour and a half or until the bird is tender. Top up the water from time to time if necessary.

CONTINUED NEXT PAGE

For the bechamel sauce:

4 tbsp BUTTER

4 tbsp FLOUR

2 cups MILK

SMALL ONION, STUDDED WITH *3* CLOVES

SMALL BAY LEAF

^{1}/$_2$ tsp SALT

^{1}/$_2$ tsp WHITE PEPPER (YOU DON'T WANT TO RUIN THE WHITE COLOUR OF THE SAUCE)

^{1}/$_4$ tsp FRESHLY GROUND NUTMEG

SMALL STICK OF CINNAMON

2 EGG YOLKS

A WHOLE NUTMEG

In a saucepan, melt the butter over a low heat then stir in the flour with a wooden spoon till it's a paste. Add all the other ingredients except the egg yolks and stir ceaselessly till the sauce is thick and smooth. Remove from the heat and stir in the egg yolks. Grate about ^{1}/$_4$ tsp nutmeg into the sauce. Just before serving, discard the onion, cinnamon stick and bay leaf. If you like a runnier sauce you can add a bit of the strained cooking fluid from the chicken.

To serve:

Carve the chicken, pile the stuffing on a platter and arrange the chicken on top. Arrange the vegetables around the chicken and pour over the béchamel sauce.

The broth can be checked for seasoning and served as soup.

GIGOT DE SEPT HEURES

SEVEN-HOUR LAMB WITH GARLIC

2 kg LEG OF MUTTON OR MATURE LAMB

LARGE BOUQUET GARNI

SALT AND FRESHLY GROUND PEPPER

3 CARROTS, PEELED AND CUT IN CHUNKS

3 SMALL TURNIPS, PEELED AND CUT IN CHUNKS

3 MEDIUM LEEKS, TRIMMED, SPLIT AND CUT IN CHUNKS

1 STICK OF CELERY, CHOPPED

3 MEDIUM ONIONS, QUARTERED

10 CLOVES OF GARLIC, CHOPPED

Tie the mutton up with string, otherwise it will fall apart with the long cooking. Place it in a roasting dish surrounded by all the other ingredients and enough water to cover it by three-quarters. Bring to the boil on top of the stove, cover and cook in a 120°C/250°F oven for an hour. Turn meat over and continue to cook, uncovered, for another four to five hours. The water should scarcely bubble and if the meat gets too dry, add more water. Remove the meat and vegetables from the roasting dish and keep warm. On top of the stove, reduce the broth to about a quarter of its original volume. Taste for seasoning, strain and serve in a jug. Remove the strings from the mutton, carve it in thick slices and serve with the vegetables.

I gave this recipe to my gourmandising friend Steve one day while standing outside the butcher shop. He came back to me with an inspired refinement. Instead of putting in the ten cloves of garlic he put in a few heads of garlic in their skins, sliced across the top, then at the end squeezed them into the sauce.

Meanwhile, into Emily's steam box went a flax basket full of kūmara and kamokamo (Māori courgette) to be followed at the last minute by pūhā and kōtaotao shoots (a sort of thistle). The creative purity of this style of cooking is very comforting. While the food was steaming, Emily produced a basket full of writhing, dusky-coloured kōura (freshwater crayfish) that had been caught in the river by the local lads. My job was to dip the basket of kōura artfully into the same hot pool they were cooking the corn in. The humidity of the afternoon sun (only mad dogs and Englishmen), combined with the heat of the percolating typhoon that I was practically immersed in, made me sweat and induced make-up melt. It melted and melted, and I tried to ignore it but the blusher and powder dripped like milky milo into the pool. Dave, who is a perfectly lovely person in every other way, but unfortunately trained at Auschwitz, showed no concern for or interest in my predicament.

'Do it again,' he said with maleficence. He waited till the wind blew the steam out of my face just long enough for the entire country to see that yes, beauty is indeed skin-deep. Another gust of steam enveloped us, but Emily is a natural woman, used to these conditions and not stupid enough to be wearing two inches (50 millimetres) of television-proof makeup.

This time I closed my eyes, but when I tried to open them I couldn't. Not many people know this, but mascara is adhesive. People who dance at discos know this; people who use very hot ovens know this; people who work in the makeup room at TVNZ know this. I didn't know this. Finally, I prized my eyes open and black tears ran down my cheeks. I looked desperately at Chris, who smiled helplessly and said:

'You're going to have to wipe it all off and start again.'

I had my TV kit that Renée at makeup had composed for me with strict instructions and a map, so wandered off to redo the whole thing. This production I have now got down to twenty-five minutes, a process that in my civilian life takes one minute. I returned to the pools of sorrow by which time sweat had broken through the mask again. We filmed a piece to camera with the help of Chris's handkerchief, dabbing the beads every time they appeared.

EMILY WITH A BASKET OF KŌURA (FRESHWATER CRAYFISH).

THE HOT POOLS AT WHAKAREWAREWA.

'Here in Whakarewarewa, people have been looking like this for hundreds of years . . .' I said to camera. Dab, dab.

'Actually, that's cooking,' said Chris.

'Here in Whakarewarewa, people have been cooking this piece of beef for hundreds of years . . .' Dab, dab.

'Cut.'

'Here in this f------ village.' Dab, dab.

'OK, OK, go and sit in the shade.'

Emily kindly offered her home near the village as a suitable venue to eat the food we had just cooked, and we found ourselves in a luxuriant, lovingly tended garden. I noticed with gratitude that the garden table was under a pergola, so I sat there going over history and whakapapa with Emily. I met her husband Bob, a fine figure of a man, and some of her grandchildren. She has seven children, nineteen grandchildren and six great-grandchildren — hard to believe when you look at her lovely, unlined face. Having a name like Mathias was a bonus in Rotorua. Everyone knew it and remembered the family business fondly.

'Oh yes, Mathias's Drapery. I used to buy all my lingerie there,' or 'I remember the Mathias boys — so handsome.'

I remember my beloved grandmother, whom I loved more than life itself, knitting bedjackets for the shop. They were pink and lacy and you wore them over your shoulders to keep away the chills while reading in bed. Grandma also knitted bedsocks that none of us numerous grandchildren could get through winter without.

'Your uncle Ian and I were on many councils and committees together,' Emily told me, 'and my girls and your Aunt Wanda's girls were guides together.'

Emily's ancestors arrived in these parts on the Te Arawa waka and her hapū is Tūhourangi-Ngāti Tarawhai. Her great-grandmother was Tuhipo Waitere, a guide at Tarawera and her aunt was the much-loved Guide Rangi. When you meet Māori, they always go into their genealogy with you: where their parents came from; what river; what mountain. Emily believes it is important to know where you came from, to know who you are. In 1927 her great-grandfather built the whare that is in the garden and it is still furnished in the

European style. Alongside the carvings, stitched panels and flax mats are Victorian dressers with photos on them, lace-covered tables with antique china, over-stuffed arm chairs and lamps. Emily is also a renowned weaver, growing her own flax in the backyard to make piupiu (flax skirts), whāriki (floor mats), tukutuku (stitched panels), korowai (cloaks) and kete (kits).

All the food had been laid out on the table and *of course* dragged out into the sun. The simply steamed food tasting slightly of the hot-pool minerals was very good, especially when eaten with hands, but the part I had really been waiting for, the bright-red kōura, was now upon me. The moment of ecstasy — could I suck the insides out of a cray and not look like Dracula's bride? I tried being delicate. Emily picked up a big, juicy one and said,

'Get into it, girl. Eat it like a Māori. First you pull the back off, then using it as a pincer remove the yucky stuff from the abdomen. Suck out the contents of the head and body, then pull the tail out of its shell. Save the best bit for last.'

This is how the French eat seafood — *nothing* is left at the end but sweet satisfaction.

'Was that Māori?' I asked, face covered in kōura, mouth involved in enthusiastic slurping noises. Not much beats the tender, melting taste of fresh crustaceans.

As we were doing the last of the dishes in Emily's kitchen, she invited me to a church barbecue they were having at her place the next day.

'I can't come, Emily,' I said, 'especially if it will be full of ministers.'

'Why?' she asked. 'You feel guilty or something?'

'No, I'm a good girl, that's why I don't need to go to church, and anyway I've told priests far too much in my life already.'

Off we go again. Where am I now? It's mauve and pink, so it must be a motel. This one had a furnace upstairs, cleverly disguised as a bedroom, and a spa pool outside. I took a long cold shower, put clean non-kōura-infested clothes on, lay down on the floor for an hour, then met the others for the tourist-hotel shoot. During these short breaks, Chris managed to sleep deeply then wake up refreshed on cue. They all tell me they have no trouble sleeping. I never sleep in a strange bed. What if there's an earthquake? What if there's an intruder? What if I don't wake up on time? What if the sheets haven't been ironed properly? How can they just sleep?

Maureen Te Rangi Rere I Waho Kingi Waaka (yes, she was Miss New Zealand in 1962) was leading the Rotorua International Māori Entertainers and dining orgy at the THC Rotorua Hotel. A large steam box had been built in the hotel garden and the hāngi was about to be lifted. Crowded around the site were Japanese, Koreans, Americans, Europeans, Australians, a few Kiwis and Dave and John bravely filming the event. Maureen, splendid in cloak and feathers and still as beautiful and elegant as ever, was explaining the kai and how it was all about sharing and aroha and how we were all one big whānau. Suddenly, Dave was charged and almost pushed over by a furious Korean in full battle gear of cameras, horn-rimmed glasses and silly hat. Dave regained his balance and kept filming. The man reasserted himself and attacked again, this time with abusive language. Just as John was about to thump him, Maureen announced that she gave the orders and everybody was to regain their positions. *Now!* My eyes were open about as wide as Chris's mouth. Apparently, we were in the way of the man's phototaking. As we all walked back into the huge dining-room, Maureen confided that she had to put up with a lot of ungracious behaviour.

The vegetables, chicken, pork and lamb from the hāngi were carved up at the buffet and laid out along with pūhā, mussels, Māori bread (made from potato water), karengo (seaweed) and eel. Other ancient native specialities such as coleslaw, salad dressing and mint sauce were there to be sneered at. Maureen said the grace.

manaakitia mai e te Ariki ēnei kai
Hei oranga mō ō mātou tinana
Whāngaia ō mātou wairua
Ki te taro o te ora
Ko Ihu Karaiti hoki tō mātou Ariki
Āmine
Bless for us this food Lord
To sustain us in body and spirit
As does the bread of life
For Jesus Christ our Lord
Amen

I piled my plate up with kūmara, potato, pūhā, lamb and eel. Next to me at our table was a lone Brazilian visitor looking desperately at the seaweed and raw, marinated fish on his plate. We got talking about Brazilian food, which I love, and soon I was back in Paris with memories of crazy Brazilian parties and warm, Portuguese accents. Meanwhile, there were lots of singing and action dancing going on up on the stage led by Maureen. She patiently and courteously explained the show to loud, insolent people who smoked when they were asked not to and seemed to be united by an extraordinary penchant for physical repulsiveness. Without warning, I was suddenly dragged up on to the stage and welcomed as a long lost daughter returned to the seat of my clan. Everyone clapped enthusiastically. It was all so natural and spontaneous I almost forgot that Dave was in my face as I was trying to keep my head down. Various tourists who were not possessed of the faintest clue as to what was about to happen to them were also tricked into getting up on the stage with the Māori wahine, there to be faced with approximately six tons of solid male tangata whenua scaring the daylights out of them. I can't hear too many waiata or hongi too many noses, so it was with great pleasure that I pressed an impressive variety of protuberances over the next ten minutes.

Māori bread uses potatoes as the leaven, the agent that produces fermentation, rather than yeast.

PARĀOA RĒWENA
MĀORI BREAD

First make the leaven

RĒWENA (LEAVEN)
3 MEDIUM POTATOES, SLICED
300 ml/1 cup WATER
600 ml/2 cups FLOUR
1 tsp SUGAR

Boil potatoes in water until soft. Cool briefly then mix in the flour and sugar to a paste. Cover and place in a warm position until the mixture has fermented.

1 kg/5 cups FLOUR
1 tsp SALT
1 tsp BAKING SODA

Sift flour and salt and make a well in the centre. Fill with rēwena and sprinkle baking soda on top. Combine and knead mixture for about ten minutes, adding a little water if the mixture is too firm. Shape into loaves or place mixture in greased loaf tins. Bake at 230°C (450°F) for 45–50 minutes.

A deep fried version (Parāoa Parai) combines flour, salt and sugar with the rēwena to make sweet, scone-like bread.

back to the motel, no sleep of course, up at six to be on the road by seven, half an hour to get the war-paint on. The wallpaper on the bathroom wall physically pained me, and as usual I looked in the mirror and said, 'How did this happen to me? I'm only seventeen years old.' My friend Steve told me to use Preparation H under my eyes to get rid of bags. I don't want to be tasteless, but a girl would really want to be sure she was using a previously unopened tube. In the very next time frame, there we were out in the middle of Lake Tarawera walking around in circles on Craig Armstrong's thirty-eight-foot launch, the originally named *Clear Water Pride*. Craig was a tall, pleasant, young man possessed of an idyllic lifestyle and a good CD collection (John Campbell, Eric Clapton, The Best of the Cream, to name but a few). He and his wife Caroline take people fishing on excursions that can go from a few hours to all day to overnight. They cater for the beginner through to the experienced angler with all equipment supplied. Tarawera is one of twelve main lakes of the region and by northern hemisphere standards they are fantastic for sports fishing. The trout grow at a phenomenal rate, in fact to trophy proportions, making fishing there amongst the best in the world.

The brief was to catch a couple of trout and cook them in the sand at Hot Water Beach. You wish. The only kind of fishing I do doesn't involve hooks and sinkers. Well . . . it does actually but I don't normally end up with a fish. Anyway, trout in these parts means business. Big business. Last year seventeen million dollars' worth of business. Not that trout is a fish to die for in my opinion, but I think it's not really cricket that one can't buy it. It's all a bit élitist what? If you don't have a boat or don't know someone with a boat then you don't eat trout.

We arrived at Hot Water Beach where someone had had the brilliant idea to cook a trout in the hot sand. As we approached in the boat, steam could be seen rising from the beach and all along the water's edge. Craig put down a ladder, the equipment was handed down and we gleefully leapt off the boat on to a REALLY HOT BEACH. It was fine if you just walked on it, but dig a toe in and it hurt. Dave's foot took approximately two minutes before the skin started coming off, so Chris figured about an hour to cook the trout, Craig reckoned

THE NECESSARY EQUIPMENT TO CATCH TROUT.

about two hours and I thought about half an hour maximum. As it turned out, it stayed in its sandy oven for an hour while I got back on the boat and pretended to catch it. Yes, in the world of television, you eat your trout and have it too. I am the only person in the universe that I know of who has caught a frozen trout, although I haven't checked *Ripley's Believe It Or Not* yet, so I don't want to be accused of harbouring illusions of grandeur.

After this extraordinary feat, I dug up the buried trout for all the world to appreciate. Needless to say, the weight of the wet, hot sand had burst the tin foil it was wrapped in and what emerged was sand pie, but what the hell, this was life, not art. Laurence actually ate it, and of course when that segment was screened lots of people called to tell me what I should really have done. Apparently, you put the trout packet in an onion sack. I also thought that as the water was so hot, I could have simply floated the trout in it without covering it with sand at all. It was still early in the day, but it was hot and sunny and I could feel the makeup starting to run slightly, so I jumped behind a bush. It was like having a skin disease that neither a hat nor an umbrella could protect.

'YOU DO THE WORK AND I'LL JUST STAND HERE AND IMPROVE MY SUNTAN,' SAID CHRIS.

WHOLE STUFFED TROUT

HOT WATER BEACH STUFFING *(OR FOR MY ALTERNATIVE, SEE RECIPE)*

MĀORI BREAD

LOTS OF CHOPPED PARSLEY

A LEMON AND A SPRIG OF FRESH MINT

ONE WHOLE TROUT, GUTTED

OLIVE OIL

MALDEN SEA SALT AND FRESHLY GROUND PEPPER

HEAVY DUTY TIN FOIL

AN ONION SACK

Find a hot water beach and run away immediately instead of doing mad things like sticking fish into it. If you can't be desisted from your path, make the stuffing by throwing the bread and parsley away so you can grab a handful of seaweed from the Japanese section of your fish shop. Mix this with some fresh dill, slices of lemon or better still lime, spring onions cut on the cross in one inch slices and lots of pink pepper corns. This stuffing is not necessarily to be eaten (although you could) but to flavour the fish.

Place stuffing into cavity of trout, brush the fish with olive oil and sprinkle with Malden sea salt and pepper. Take a sheet of tin foil large enough to fold over the fish, and close the three open sides by folding over three times to ensure that it doesn't burst open. Place in an onion sack. Dig a shallow hole in the sand, put your package in and cover gently with sand. Go away and drink Rosé with your friends for about three-quarters of an hour, depending on the size of the fish.

It is hoped you will remember where you have buried the fish. When I was in Greece, my friends and I would always bury our bottle of Retsina in the cold water just beyond the shore. When we went out to get it we could never find it, but we always found other people's, which of course we drank. If you dig where you thought you left the trout and find a bottle of Retsina, I suggest you go back to the boat, have a cup of tea and a lie down and try again later.

I think the stuffed trout would be ideal eaten with a salad of rocket and cherry tomatoes sprinkled with olive oil and balsamic vinegar.

Much more successful and delicious was filleted trout smoked in a wok on the back of Craig's launch. This was Laurence's invention, and it worked astoundingly well. My friend Anna who spends a lot of time on her launch says the only cooking utensil you need on a boat is a wok; chuck the rest out. We fixed up our trusty little gas burner as I tried very hard not to fall off the stern. Given to large gestures, it's easy for me to lose balance. As with Peter Thornley's Smoked Peppers, the ideal cooking situation would be in one of those flash barbecues that have covers. That way you don't smoke up your kitchen and have the neighbours call the fire brigade.

WOOD-SMOKED TARAWERA TROUT

2 FILLETS OF FRESH TROUT

MALDEN SEA SALT AND FRESHLY GROUND PEPPER

1 tbsp BROWN SUGAR

OLIVE OIL

TIN FOIL

MANUKA SHAVINGS

FRESH HERBS SUCH AS THYME, SAGE, ROSEMARY, LEMON BALM

Remove the tiny bones that run down the centre of the fillets with eyebrow tweezers or small pliers. Sprinkle the fillets with salt, pepper, sugar and olive oil. (If you like a firmer texture, sprinkle the trout with salt and leave in the fridge overnight or for a few hours to bring out some of the moisture. Wipe off the excess salt before smoking.) Line the wok with two layers of tin foil and on top place the manuka and herbs. Cover with a grill (we used a round cake rack) and place the trout on top. Cover the whole thing securely with a lid or foil and wrap the edge with a damp, rolled-up tea towel.

Turn the flame up to high until the wood starts smoking, then lower the heat and smoke gently for about twenty minutes.

We served the fish with a generous helping of steamed asparagus, red pepper salad and a bottle of Fumé Blanc.

I can't tell you how awful it was sitting on the deck of *Clear Water Pride* eating that trout and sipping that wine with Craig, while the crew watched and filmed and salivated. The lake was still, it was a perfect day, and you don't even have to be behind the wheel to drive the thing. Why can't cars be like that?

On the way back to the motel, we stopped at the hot pools at Wai-o-tapu to see the result of the fire locked up in the central volcanic plateau. This is a very powerful landscape, in fact, it's like a moonscape from a science-fiction movie: pale, white, silent, ethereal, steamy and very sulphurous. In the middle of it all is the Champagne Pool covering 4000 metres of a sinter-lined nine-hundred-year-old explosion crater. The gas bubbles rising to the surface are harmless carbon dioxide, making it look like Champagne. The alkaline chloride water contains gold, silver, arsenic and mercury as well as lots of other minerals. I saw a boiled birdie but didn't think even mustard sauce could make up for the poison in the Champagne stock. Opposite the pool, which is about 76°C, you can see three distinct layers of soil. The upper layer comes from the pool and the second layer comes from the Taupo eruption 1800 years ago. Other pools are eggshell-blue, some are mud, some are pale sage-green and one wanders around as if in a dream, longing to leap into the milky depths.

■

If you've ever wondered what millions of sperm might look like and you didn't see the Woody Allen movie, go to the Eastern Region Fish and Game Trout Hatchery, where a very pretty redhead called Debbie will let you touch them. Twenty thousand healthy youngsters are released for a life of Russian roulette with every bite they take. Eggs are collected from selected rainbow hens (did you know that's what a lady trout is called?) from the spawning runs in the Lake Tarawera system. The breeding programme selects fish that have performed well in the wild. Characteristics such as faster growth and older age at maturity, which allow growth to a larger size, are favoured. The seasonal timing of spawning is under quite tight genetic control, then the little darlings are incubated in huge trays, each one containing 10,000 eggs (don't even ask me how you count them). As they get bigger they get transferred to holding ponds, the largest one holding 35,000 trout. These ponds are very cold −11°C, which is great for trout health. On their first birthday, they are released back from whence they came to be trolled, harled, spun and fly-fished from boats, from the lakeshore and from the river.

Because I had decided to have a big hair day, it was drizzling rain, and for this reason Chris insisted that I interview Debbie at the holding pond outside. Debbie and I both have red hair and freckles, and within minutes we looked like Christmas trees covered in fairy lights. It was first thing in the morning and normally I've had more time to get to know my victim. Also, I was not totally awake yet in the technical sense of the word and couldn't work myself up into a lather over some wet fish. I am constantly thinking up ways to help the interviewee relax and be as wonderful on screen as they are off. I noticed that Debbie had a packet of tobacco in her pocket, so suggested we sit on a nearby bench. Talking to people about everything save the subject of the interview is a good trick, a hip flask can help and sharing a roll-your-own is definitely a way of establishing trust. We sat in the drizzle, sucking on fags (I did it only for the job) and pretending we were in an Alpine ad. It wasn't hard considering the stunning scenery — beautiful, calm and green. By the time Dave and John were ready, Debbie and I had bonded and didn't want to approach the camera without fags hanging out of our mouths. Needless to say, Debbie responded very well to the 'And so Debbie, how big is big?' question.

Our last shoot before driving back to Auckland was at Rainbow Springs, where trout are on display at all stages of growth. This showpiece has made itself attractive to both thousands of visitors and to thousands of trout which find life in the cool, clear spring water is too good to leave. I also had to be seen driving the red Avis car through the entrance.

'We've reccied the area for 500 metres for ditches, Peta,' said Chris. 'Do you think you can drive along this straight stretch of road?'

'Very funny.'

A QUIET BACKWATER ON THE
WAITAMATA HARBOUR.

auckland

la découverte d'un mets nouveau fait plus pour le bonheur du genre humain que la découverte d'une étoile — the discovery of a new food gives more happiness to the human race than the discovery of a star

BRILLAT-SAVARIN

Surely the most incandescent star in our culinary sky in Auckland must be the recent discovery of Japanese food. I was first introduced to *sushi* when I was living in Vancouver in 1974 and instantly became addicted. The flavours and textures were so clean and light in comparison to Western food, and I loved sitting on the floor with my shoes off and eating either with my fingers or with chopsticks. It was only after a few years that I realised the warm *sake* served to me in innocent little cups was at least 16 per cent proof and that may have been why I enjoyed my outings *chez les Japonais* so much. But first things first.

Laurence called me a week before the shoot to say he was having difficulty making progress with Seamart. We wanted to film their hugely popular, eclectic fish shop on Fanshaw Street and hoped to interview the owner, Vojislav Krtolica. With a simple name like that, I couldn't see why Laurence was having trouble communicating.

'Nobody speaks English. They speak Chinese, Tongan, Croatian and Korean,' he bemoaned, 'and Voja is being elusive. I'm not getting anywhere.'

It was then I remembered that my friend Graeme Halse, fisherman and footballer extraordinaire, was their lawyer. I felt sure he could help, and I wasn't wrong. Graeme got on the blower and organised a meeting between Voja, Laurence, him and me the next day at 4 pm. Helen, Voja's lovely office manager, said she would try to make sure he was there but she couldn't promise anything.

'Maybe he'll turn up, maybe he won't.'

It's a well-documented scientific fact that if four people decide to meet at a certain hour in fishy circumstances, something will go wrong. We defied statistics and all turned up at the shark-fin counter at the same time. I was on double lipstick duty, Laurence was on obsequiousness alert and the gorgeous Graeme turned up with a bottle of Chivas. Once again, it was proven that whisky and hanging out is the secret to successful research. It may in fact be the secret to everything but we'll talk about that another time. We crammed into Voja's little office and talked about everything except fish — gambling, Paris, the one that got away, the state of English soccer and wine. Voja told me the story of how he won some money in a lottery and spent the whole day driving around Paris in a taxi, gambling till he had not one centime left. I found this story deeply moving and wished I had been there. We all snacked on still warm, freshly smoked fish straight from the smoker out back, spread out on newspaper on the office desk. As we left, I confirmed with Voja that he would let me interview him.

'No,' he said with his thick accent, 'I'm not talking in front of the camera. Get someone else.'

'I want *you* and make sure you have a clean apron on,' I smiled.

'Have some more whisky.'

'No, thank you, and I will bend you to my will,' I replied.

'I don't think so.'

'See you tomorrow.'

We arrived the next day trailing all our equipment with cameraman Dave and sound man John. I was wearing a scarf in my hair and a skirt closely resembling a tutu. Voja thought I looked French and immediately offered me a cigarette. Dave filmed eels, crayfish, *sushi*, squid, orange roughy and scampi while Voja tried to escape. Everything that I adore was there — Japanese food garnishes, ling bladders, Morton Bay bugs, oysters, monkfish, seaweed, people screaming in foreign languages, noise, serious buyers that knew exactly what they were looking for and, of course, dried shark's fins at $50 for 100 grams. And people *pay the price* willingly. It's hard to believe you're in Auckland — almost all the faces are Asian and Pacific

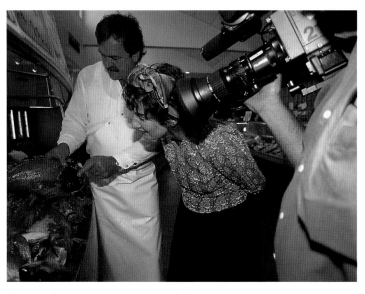

VOJA AND PETA DISCUSSING THE DAY'S CATCH.

Island. They walk around with inverted plastic bags on their hands looking for the freshest whole fish. Either they have it gutted and filleted by the executioners behind the counter or they take it home and do it themselves. Chris grabbed Voja and stuck him next to the whole fish table in the middle of the room, stuck me next to him and said, 'Talk.'

As I talked and Voja froze, Dave was having trouble getting one person who was five foot four (about 1.63 metres) and another person who was six foot four (about 1.93 metres) into the same frame. I looked like I was interviewing the ceiling and he looked like he was talking to the floor. He didn't like it but he did it. His English was sort of OK, but I didn't think the rest of New Zealand would understand it (excepting those who live in Kumeu), so I repeated everything he said. I didn't know what he said, but I repeated it anyway. I think he said the *sushi* rage came about because the food is healthy, it's fashionable and he couldn't understand how people could eat raw fish anyway.

Walk around Auckland City centre these days and you'll be hard pressed to find a fish and chip shop. The old Anglo-Saxon food traditions have long been cast aside in favour of the food of the Mediterranean, Asia, Thailand, Hong Kong . . . but now fish is definitely back on the menu, only the wrapping around it's not newsprint but rice. We hit the *Sushi* Factory in Vulcan Lane where they have a *sushi* robot and you pluck little bowls of food off a conveyor belt for your lunch. I was in ecstasy at the thought of having to eat this stuff as part of my job, and Dave was going pale just looking at it.

'I want a pie and a custard slice,' he said.

'Try it, Dave,' I enthused, 'you'll love it. It's only seaweed, cold omelette and raw octopus. And guess what? It's your lunch.'

'I want to leave.'

'Don't be ridiculous — it's good for you.'

'That's made my mind up. I knew there was something weird about this whole set-up.'

One of the best things about eating raw fish is the green *wasabi* or Japanese horseradish and the pickled ginger. These condiments were originally served to stop food poisoning from fish that wasn't in its first bloom of youth, but now, even though *sushi* is famous for being desperately fresh, people still pile on the *wasabi*. The word *sushi* is a corruption of *sumeshi* meaning vinegared rice. In Japan, *sushi* bars are popular at lunchtime when raw fish is freshest.

I sat at the bar watching with hawk eye the little plates of delicacies moving past on the conveyor belt — raw salmon on rice, raw marinated slices of beef, *Sushi* Rolls, fresh fruit cut into artistic pieces, *sashimi* (slices of raw fish) and seaweed-wrapped *tofu*. The choice seemed endless and the

PETA AT THE *SUSHI* FACTORY.

plates piled up beside me, their colour determining their price. At the end of the shoot, the whole crew dived into the delicacies, including Dave who nibbled carefully.

'Why do you like this stuff so much?' he asked.

'It reminds me of making love,' I replied, mouth full.

'I beg your pardon?'

'Yeah, you know. To love the taste of something is to give yourself up to it. There is no withholding, no dragging of one's feet. It's a sort of voluptuous surrender,' I waxed.

'You what?' asked Laurence.

'Sounds OK to me,' said Chris.

'Are they all like this in France or did you have a dodgy upbringing?' asked Dave.

'Remove yourself from my personal space, infidel, and remember your tongue is a wet place and it is liable to slip,' I replied sweetly.

'Peta,' said Chris, 'how'd you like to do some vox pops outside the *sushi* takeaway on Lorne Street?'

'Sure. What are they? Do they hurt? Do I need a uniform?'

We hung out outside the takeaway bar on the street, where I wasted a year of my life running a café, shoving the microphone into innocent buyer's faces and asking them why they liked *sushi*. This is what they said:

'Raw fish — yuck (fingers down mouth).'

'My boyfriend doesn't like it but I do.'

'It's aesthetic — like eating art.'

'It's healthy and has no fat.'

'I like the taste.'

'How much are you paying me for this interview?'

'It's light, easy to eat and inexpensive.'

'I'm not interested, thank you.'

'Can't stand the stuff — only eat it for the *wasabi*.'

'Don't film me with my glasses on.'

Everywhere we went people seemed to be eating *sushi*. This space was selling pink cardies last time I walked down here. The office workers who have always thrilled to the taste of pies, lamingtons and coke are now sipping sparkling water and wolfing down artistic health food, including fish that's never seen a flame in its life. This can only end in happiness. My tutu consisted of four layers of silk tulle and lots of fresh air. It was a windy day and if I had legs like Elle it would have been great but I don't so it wasn't.

On top of that, because this is my home town, I kept bumping into my friends. It usually happened when John had his hands down my front or up my back in what he called wiring me up but what I called harassment in the workplace. My friends, being the discreet, measured people they are, invariably burst into loud laughter and tooting and shouting across traffic lights. Everywhere we went, we got people wanting us to promote them — from the Angus Steak House to the made-to-measure shirt shop. Aucklanders were definitely not slow in coming forward. Dave now maintained he felt sick after his *sushi* lunch but quickly perked up when we let him sit down for a custard slice.

One of the things that saved me from despair when I was working on Lorne Street was the discovery of Café Rikka on Queen Street just above the Town Hall. This minuscule *sushi* bar only seated eight people at two tables and half a dozen people around the bar. It was known that the service was very slow so you had to arrive on the dot of twelve or be for ever lost. There is a saying that opines the closest we ever come to perfection is when we write our CVs, but I always feel I'm on the way when I eat Yoshito Okada's lunch special. His fish is incredibly fresh and the rice is always moist and sweet. Yoshi first came to New Zealand on holiday and loved it for its beauty and lack of crowds, then returned seven years ago to live here. He and his beautiful wife Manami have now opened another, larger restaurant on Drake Street behind Victoria Park Market. My friends and I ate there after an opening one night, and the service was in the same vein as the original Rikka, in fact it was so bad one of our group never actually got fed at all. Not one to hold a grudge as the food really is special there, I suggested to Chris that we include them in our segment.

We climbed through a hole in the wall into the restaurant, and every staff member in the restaurant made it clear they had no idea who we were or what we wanted. Thankfully, Manami serenely wafted in, as tiny, mysterious and gracious as ever, to help. Yoshi began to lay out his ingredients and the tools of the trade — bamboo leaves, scampi heads, miniature rafts, cherry blossom leaves, bamboo pyramids, salmon roe, snapper, squid, trevally, tuna and John Dory. Slowly, all the staff lined up along the back of the room to watch, Manami started being bossy according to Yoshi, and Yoshi was not being creative enough according to Manami. He spoke very bad English, but I thought if he continued to be relaxed we could

probably cope. You wish. The moment Dave said 'rolling', Yoshi became completely paralytic with stage-fright and remained in an acute state of flight and fright throughout the whole shoot.

He almost sliced his hand off several times, sweated profusely, got lockjaw and couldn't speak Japanese, English or any other language and behaved as if he had never seen rice before in his life. When I asked him a question (I started off with non-negotiable ones like — what is your name?) he stared wide-eyed at me, so I gave up the question and non-answer routine and we opted for the Zen solution — silent demonstration. Eventually, a pretty redhead called Jo who was our standby translator was asked to facilitate, not because of the language problem but because our chef was nearing the last stages of rigor mortis.

We three sat down at a table in front of the stunningly presented, succulent *sashimi* that Yoshi had prepared. He had created a Japanese garden of raw fish, bamboo bridge, leaves and summer flowers and another pastoral scene achieved with crushed ice, different coloured fish and delicate little bamboo leaves. He also made a California Roll, which is quite flash as the *nori* or seaweed paper is on the inside rather than the outside. I asked him questions like, 'So Yoshi, what's so special about *sushi*?' when what I really wanted to say was, 'I'll never do this to you again and do you know that my radio mike is realigning my kidneys?' He replied in Japanese to Jo, who translated to the camera. And so this little three-pronged crown of thorns went on till Chris looked happy and released us from the merry-go-round. We were all so relieved the man had actually talked that we dived on to the *sushi* and *sake* to fill up the anxiety hormones in our stomachs. Dave, strangely enough, had got over his 'dodgy stomach' and was into the *sashimi* for the second time in one day. Once they had packed up, Yoshi began to talk, telling me that he had trained for seven years in Japan under a teacher who always insisted that each dish be a picture. For him, food is really art and he is giving something of himself with every dish he prepares.

SUSHI ROLL

1 cup SHORT GRAIN RICE

1 tbsp JAPANESE VINEGAR (OR WHITE WINE VINEGAR, ADDING A TSP OF SUGAR)

1/2 tsp SALT

NORI (SEAWEED PAPER)

WASABI

VERY FRESH RAW FISH, CUT INTO THIN STRIPS

PICKLED DAIKON RADISH

COOKED CARROT STICKS

BAMBOO PADDLE FOR SPREADING RICE

BAMBOO ROLLING MAT

SOY SAUCE

PICKLED GINGER

To cook the rice, wash it under running cold water for ten minutes. Place it in a pot and cover with cold water to one centimetre above the level of the rice. Bring to the boil, lower the heat to a simmer and cover tightly. When there is no more liquid in the pot, the rice is cooked. It takes about twenty minutes and the consistency is sticky. Melt together the vinegar (and sugar if using white wine vinegar) and salt and pour over the cooked rice. Allow to cool.

CONTINUED NEXT PAGE

that evening we had a shoot at the Carlton Hotel, kindly facilitated by Allyson Gofton. Upstairs they have a Japanese quarter comprising the Tatami room for formal dining and Katsura for *teppanyaki*. We walked into a quiet, ordered world of softly spoken, Kimono-clad waitresses and the clean, simple lines of Japanese interiors. I relished the idea of removing my shoes as is customary but didn't relish the idea of everyone else doing it. The Tatami room is a gracious space closed off by sliding screens, called *shoji*, with panels in them that can be raised to reveal the snowflakes falling in winter and the cherry blossoms in summer. The decor was simple, subtle and calm, the low table surrounded by a moat where you put your legs. In Japan, you sit on mats on the floor, but these

Have a tall glass of water ready to dip your paddle in, to make spreading the rice easier.

Lay a sheet of *nori* on the mat and cover with rice to both edges and to within a centimetre of the front and back edges. Towards the front spread a line of *wasabi* and on top of that place a line of fish, a line of radish and a line of carrot.

With the help of the mat, roll up the *sushi* and give the roll a gentle squeeze to make sure it has all stuck together. Slice into bite-size pieces and eat immediately with extra *wasabi*, soy sauce and pickled ginger.

Sushi Rolls don't keep, so they must be made just before you intend to eat them.

CALIFORNIA ROLL

In this gorgeous variation, you spread the rice on the *nori* and sprinkle the rice with sesame seeds. Then you flip the whole thing on to the mat, which you have now covered with a damp cloth, so the seeds are on the outside. Spread on *wasabi* followed by mayonnaise, avocado, prawn or crab meat and cucumber. To roll up, use your hands and the damp cloth to stop everything sticking to you. This is a much fatter roll than the regular one, so stuff lots of filling into it.

rooms have now been adapted to European needs, hence the moats and special seats with backs on them for comfort. This room is used for high-level entertaining, business meetings and formal occasions. On one wall is the *kakejiku* or painting that designates the head of the table.

For the filming of our *teppanyaki* dinner at the flamboyant hands of chef David Foo, five other people had been invited to join me. In the voice-over, the script said they were my friends. I had never seen them before in my life except for one person — the Silver Fox himself. I couldn't believe my luck that the inimitable, debonair Greg Stanaway was one of the chosen ones and immediately ordered him to sit next to me, thus ensuring zesty, mettlesome company. An old friend of my brother's, Greg and I had enjoyed many social occasions together over the years, and this one proved no less enjoyable than the others. Unfortunately, if we thought we were going to enjoy a *sake*-fuelled Bacchanal we were sadly mistaken. We were permitted ONE little jug (*tokkuri*) of *Gekkeikan sake*. Greg poured my *sake* and I poured his into our little porcelain cups (*sakazuki*), as is the custom.

TEPPANYAKI CHEF, DAVID FOO, AT WORK.

Teppanyaki means grill plate and it is a solid steel grill that can reach very high temperatures. This style of cooking is not, strictly speaking, Japanese — the origins are thought to have been Hawaiian from the 1960s, started by the Japanese who lived there. The food was barbecued because of Americans' reluctance to eat raw meat. We sat around the grill, wiped our hands on the cool, refreshing towels provided and waited for the show to begin. There's no business like show business and David was a true cultural entertainer with a flair for tingling the taste buds. A little bowl of shredded beef with a sharp sauce came first, followed by an acrobatic display of knife juggling. I wondered what my insurance policy was with TVNZ should any of this knife flying rearrange my hair-do. David asked who liked garlic, we all shot our hands up, so a huge handful was thrown on to the grill and sautéed with much flashing and clashing of utensils. He kept this crispy, nutty-tasting stimulant on the side ready for flavouring when and as desired.

Just as I was about to pass on some incredibly stupid joke to Greg, a flying prawn's tail landed in my bowl, a by-product of some creative sautéeing on the grill. The pepper mill got whirled around, vodka, lemon juice and *yumyum* sauce got swished in and suddenly there was a plate of tender giant prawns in front of us. Shrieks all round except from Greg who remained calm. Next David whipped up fillets of salmon with sesame seeds and oil, followed by fried rice and soup. There was a strict protocol to be followed as with all Japanese eating, and being a recovered good Catholic girl I still had a keen feel for ritual. This was no rice *ordinaire*, needless to say. We watched spellbound as David threw the eggs in the air to be caught and bisected on the edge of his slice, swirled around on the grill and rolled up into an omelette. Next, he fried up the rice with vodka and hand-minced vegetables, put this into a corner of the grill from the other side and indulged in a lightning-speed shredding of omelette into the pile of rice. Greg and I leaned back as the pieces flew through the air and somehow found their way into bowls that were somersaulted from David to us. We all burst into wild applause.

You might be forgiven for suspecting that the show was over as we had already been at the table for at least an hour. But no, this is what is so wonderful about *teppanyaki* eating — it takes ages and you never feel stuffed but you don't leave feeling hungry either. Slices of tender beef grilled with garlic, *yumyum* and lemon were followed by chicken fillets done the same way. This may not be the order in which the food is normally cooked, but this was how it happened with us, probably because of the demands of the camera. Sadly, the evening did come to a close eventually and I drank Japanese tea while the crew were fed by David.

queenstown

l'ordre des boissons est des plus tempérées aux plus fumeuses et aux plus parfumées — the order of drinks is from the most temperate to the most aromatic and fragrant

BRILLAT-SAVARIN

this was our first shoot of the new year, so everyone was relaxed and tanned after the holidays. Laurence picked me up at Queenstown Airport on a still, blue, perfect mid-January evening. He and Chris had gone from normal winter pallor to deep golden and were now flashing kneecaps and elbows. I had gone from pale freckles to what looked like a radiation outbreak. We drove through the remarkable (get it?) mountains then through Arrowtown, which looked like a village for vertically challenged people. It was like driving through a painting. As Queenstown sits on the 45° south parallel, that puts it half-way between the equator to the north and Antarctica to the south. The weather from these two major influences is directly responsible for its hot summers and very cold winters. A remote, stunningly beautiful place, Queenstown sits at the base of the Southern Alps nestling alongside a sheltered bay of Lake Wakatipu.

Presently we came across a village called Millbrook — our humble lodgings. It was as if, upon being placed at the feet of the majestic mountains, the whole village had blanched in tender admiration. This was way above our normal standard of accommodation, and I wondered what hoops had been jumped through to arrange it. One arrives by way of an avenue of elm and oak trees planted by the property's original owners. Millbrook is a sporting resort and playground for the well-heeled complete with eighteen-hole golf course designed by Bob Charles, tennis court, swimming pool and extremely fat duvets, so what were we doing there? The beds were as big as my home in Ponsonby, a fact everyone noticed, all lamenting that they had no one to share them with. The villas were a cadenza of bleached, colour-washed blues, beiges and creams with crisp, white bed linen edged in lace, plush pillows and a flush of blue cushions. French doors opened out to spectacular views from both the bedroom and the dining-room. It was a palette of perfection. Formally a wheat farm dating back to the 1860s, Millbrook is still dotted with rustic stone buildings.

We all dined together at an Italian restaurant on the property, housed in the restored mill-house. It was a happy reunion with our Dunedin crew of John and Barrie, and certain parties immediately fell into their routine of wondering just how far room service would go as they watched a girl leaning provocatively over the wall outside to admire the ducks. A few sheep and gumboot jokes, and we settled

down to a serious production meeting, which involved recounting the most dangerous ski stories, discussing turning Millbrook into an old-age home for ourselves, studying how many olive stones can fit on the base of an upturned wine glass and handing out 'provisional rundowns', which loosely translated meant 'we'll hit the Queenstown Food and Wine Festival and cruise'.

It was just as well we had a luxurious night's sleep for filming the festival turned out to be incredibly hard work because of the heat and the millions of different things going on. On the festival menu was this statement: 'Haggis, turnips and potatoes. Definitely a Scottish theme washed down with some bagpipe playing.' This is possibly the most extraordinary menu item I've ever read. It took me ages to figure out how you wash a theme down with bagpipes, and quite frankly it made me uncomfortable to think about it. In fact, the more I thought about it the more I realised I should take action. We let pseudo sentences like that go by all the time. I'm asking people to mobilise and join the fight against outrageous claims by writing to their member of parliament DEMANDING funding for a study to for God's sake find out what kind of turnips and potatoes require a wind instrument, which has more things sticking out of it than a colostomy bag, to wash them down.

The festival was held in a field on Robins Road surrounded by mountains and azure sky, and high above us people were parapenting in what looked like banana skins. I thanked my lucky stars that I was doing a food show, secure in the knowledge that the chief would never ask me to fly in a banana skin. More about that later. There wasn't a lot for me to do while they were setting up the festival — no victims to torture — so I went for a walk in the town.

That took five minutes. Touristy and awful. I watched while the crew filmed people spitting into two buckets — the wine judges Peter Munslow and Simon Waghorn were judging the twelve wines that had been submitted in brown paper bags. I can never watch people spitting without wanting to slap them, so I waited outside.

By this time the festival was in full swing and most people had set up their tents and stalls. I have to say, for a festival that's main focus was wine, the food stalls were very, very good. The Millbrook chef, Roland Schibig, was busily cooking the most divine snack of Espresso-Marinated Lamb fillets that he was grilling then placing on

ESPRESSO-SPIKED LAMB

FOR THE LAMB:

600 g LAMB LOINS

1/2 tsp CUMIN

1/2 tsp CURRY POWDER

1/2 tsp GROUND CORIANDER

2 tsp CHINESE FIVE SPICE

2 tsp BROWN SUGAR

SALT AND FRESHLY GROUND BLACK PEPPER

2 cups TRIPLE STRENGTH ITALIAN ESPRESSO

Toss the lamb loins in the spices, sugar and salt, then pour over the espresso and marinate for twenty-four hours in the fridge.

FOR THE ROASTED TOMATO SAUCE:

1 kg RIPE TOMATOES

1 tsp SUGAR

2 tbsp OLIVE OIL

Cut the tomatoes in half and roast them quickly on a very high heat in the oven. Place them in a saucepan and stir them around a bit with the sugar and the olive oil.

CONTINUED NEXT PAGE

top of slices of *baguette* with roasted tomato sauce and marinated cucumber. You may think it odd to marinate lamb in coffee, but then Roland is Swiss and they do mad things over there, but they're also the best-trained chefs in the world so I decided to trust him. So did hundreds of other people at the festival because the classy, well-organised Millbrook stall was surrounded all day by happy revellers. (My editor has since told me that she commonly adds a cup of black coffee when she roasts lamb — it's a Jamaican tradition. The lamb doesn't have a coffee taste but is left very succulent.)

The simplest sauce in the world, made special by the caramelising of the tomatoes in the oven.

FOR THE MARINATED CUCUMBER:

1 cup RICE VINEGAR

1 tsp FRESH, CHOPPED GINGER

1 tbsp SUGAR

1 CUCUMBER, SEEDED AND CUT INTO MATCH STICKS

Bring the vinegar, sugar and ginger to a boil and pour over the cucumber. The cucumber can just sit in that marinade till you're ready to use it.

TO PUT THE WHOLE THING TOGETHER:

8 SLICES OF OLIVE FOCACCIA IN BAGUETTE SHAPE

Remove the loins from the marinade and wrap them into coils, securing them with toothpicks. Sauté for four minutes on each side. While they are cooking grill the focaccia slices. Place a dollop of tomato sauce on each slice, top with a lamb coil and a little pile of cucumber.

Consume with a bottle of Gibbston Valley Pinot Gris 1995 (which won the wine-tasting competition at the festival).

this was the fourth Queenstown Wine and Food Festival, the aim being to show the rest of the country that Central Otago has come of age. Everybody exhibiting was up for an award: best overall stand; best wine; best food. With more than a hundred eating establishments in Queenstown alone, the innovation level was bound to be high. There was the largest *Mille Feuille* ever made which was a fraud in my opinion as it was simply a whole bunch of short *Mille Feuilles* joined together. It's a revolting thought at any length. There was the crab-racing competition by the Nanami *Sushi* restaurant wherein either the winner or the loser got eaten. The Boardwalk restaurant were doing Yakitori Chicken and Crayfish Open Sandwiches that they could barely keep up with (and which won the best food competition). They also did Tempura Prawns, Spare Ribs, Steamed Mussels, Nelson Oysters with Shallot and Red-Wine Vinegar Sauce and Grilled Prawns.

My favourite Whitestone cheeses were there, having won in 1994 the award with the longest name in the history of the world: The Print-Pac Food Awards Massey University Enterprise Award. Amongst others, they make Farmhouse, Brie, Airedale and Blue in

QUEENSTOWN WINE AND FOOD FESTIVAL — A GREAT DAY OUT!

that enigmatic 'art of controlled spoilage' called cheese making. We couldn't keep away from their samplings and they were such charming people. There was an Indian stall, a smoked-salmon stall, a coffee stall, a haggis stall, a stall selling raw salmon and warm potatoes (which was very weird) and many other innovative fast foods to choose from. You paid for them with the festival currency called nuggets, which I was disappointed to find were in paper, not gold. I thought we should have had to dig around in streams for them.

The heat was unbelievable, even at eleven o'clock in the morning, so I was glad when Chris suggested a sequence that was situated in the shade of the nugget tent. I was wearing a red sundress, so as is entirely correct for someone who is dressed nicely, I was asked to get on.my hands and knees and crawl around in the dirt under the table. Being nicely dressed is, of course, a matter of opinion. When my mother's friends are being nice they call it sophisticated tat and when they're being nasty they say, 'But Ann, she must be earning so much money. Why is she wearing rags from the Salvation Army?' Normal. I was supposed to be pretending to steal the nuggets and hide them in a very secret place where they would never be found. I crawled under the nugget-seller's counter, found a box full of them and stuffed handfuls down the front of my dress. Needless to say, when I stood up they all fell straight through and on to the grass.

'Need any more cleavage shots, boss?' asked John.

'No, I think we've got quite enough of that, thank you, John,' Chris replied.

There was a profusion of jazz bands of varying quality, but no *real* jazz like Blue Train or Nathan Haines. Theatre sports were there being wonderfully silly all day. I got fined by one of their policemen for being under the limit of alcohol consumption. Later on, I was offered some delicious 'Chateaux Cardboardx' from a man wearing a cardboard box. The wine was described as 'a cheeky blend of things found around the house. It has the bouquet of a shotputter's armpit. It's an *appellation contrôlée* designed to open up the sluices at both ends. Enjoy it if you can.' The spigot was at a level I'll leave to your imagination, from which emerged a uric-coloured wine.

We did some vox pops where I got asked more questions than I asked:

ME: Why did you come today, sir?

INEBRIATE: Why are you wearing all that makeup in this heat at an open air festival?

ME: Hello, madam. What do you think of the festival?

MADAM: Could you hold my wine for me while I go to the toilet?

ME: Hello, girls. Are you enjoying yourselves?

GIRLS: We've been looking at you all day. How did you get your hair to go that colour?

ME: So, which wines did you like the best?

DIPSOMANIAC: Woops. Sorry about your dress. Do you mind if I just lie down? (Crash)

Rippon Wines were there with their famous organic Pinot Noir. Morven Hill and Dunstan Vineyards of Kawarau Estate were there. They also operate under BIO-GRO certified principles. The hardest person I tried to interview that day was a wine writer whose attitude was so ungracious and rude that we actually had to drop the idea and think of something else. I suggested Pauline Haslemore, a pretty, bubbly woman who was probably much more knowledgeable about Central Otago wines and certainly thirty-seven kilometres ahead in the friendliness department. Pauline was the festival co-ordinator and an absolutely perfect person for the job with her endless good humour and helpfulness. I had to interview her on a hillside in the searing sun overlooking the festival site, and we spent the entire interview trying not to slide down the slope.

Next we dragged our increasingly drooping selves over to the Magic Box chefs' cook off — the big event of the day. A large tent had been set up as a kitchen and it was time for the senior chefs to strut their stuff. This was the big time — these experienced chefs could turn a few uninspiring ingredients into gastronomic *chef d'ouvres*. I had looked in earlier on at the apprentice chefs who were all in desperate states of nervousness with their parents looking on. Chairs were lined up in front of the cooking tables for the spectators, and to one side was the judge's table. The eight chefs were provided with two buckets, one with water and one for rubbish, two gas rings, a power point and a box with fifteen unknown ingredients. Each had an hour to create a dinner for two.

The heat was even worse in these tents as there was no cross ventilation. The chefs were more or less calm, dripping in sweat and doing all sorts of things with a rump of lamb. The meal I liked the best was cooked by a chef who was tipped to win but in the end didn't. He covered the plates with a *jus* and on top of that placed a ring made from cooked slices of carrot. Into this ring was stuffed *polenta* and sautéed, finely julienned vegetables, on top of which sat slices of rare, pan-fried lamb. It was beautiful, he knew when to stop and, according to the girl who bought it, it tasted wonderful. One plate was given to the judges to analyse and the other was auctioned off to support a good cause.

Central Otago wines really are quite different, partially because they are the southern-most in the world and partially because the growers and makers are such determined trail blazers. They mirror previous pioneers who turned over the very same soil in pursuit of gold. Nowhere else in New Zealand are vineyards found in such diverse and rugged locations — clinging to the sides of steep river gorges, flowing gracefully to the shores of lakes and sprouting from jagged, rocky hillsides. Only fifteen years ago, the Queenstown area was considered too cold for grapes. Against all predictions, these properties are now producing delicately flavoured boutique wines from 'Pinot Noir', 'Reisling', 'Sauvignon Blanc', 'Chardonnay', 'Pinot Gris' and 'Merlot' grapes. It turned out that the cold winters, hot, dry summers and cool, sunny autumns provide near-perfect growing conditions. Also, Central Otago vineyards are the highest and furthest from the sea in New Zealand. I found out later that a Frenchman called Jean Desiré Feraud had actually grown grapes and many other fruits and vegetables near Clyde in the 1860s and 70s. He produced award-winning wines, then disappeared and no one knows what happened to him.

At the end of the day, we dragged back to our vehicles, passing young men on the grass in states of supine, wine-fuelled comas, their friends tenderly preventing them from inhaling substances other than air. I arrived at Millbrook with sticky clothes, swollen feet and aching legs, all remedied by a long, cold shower and a lie down on the floor. I knew Laurence would be sipping his G and T in his villa and Chris would probably be asleep. Later on, some of us who had the energy struggled up the slope to the Clubhouse restaurant on the property. The doors were thrown open to the stone terrace, where one could listen to cicadas scratching their wings, watch the ducks in the pond and sing with the birds. We, of course, did no such thing. We busied ourselves with finding the most isolated table against a wall and proceeded to order things that weren't on the menu and not obey instructions from the *maître d'hôtel*, a delicious man called Sebastian whose arrogance was excelled only by his sardonic humour. I instantly fell in love with him and wanted to marry him, then leave him, until I remembered I was married to someone else.

None of this changed the fact that we were meant for each other. He understood exactly how to play the power and control game, saving himself every time from obnoxiousness with his elegance and intelligence. When the dessert menus arrived, I asked for one each.

'There aren't enough to go around, madam,' he said.

'I'm not interested. We all wish a menu each, please. We don't do sharing,' I explained.

'You will share and that's how I wish it,' he snipped.

I squirmed with pleasure. Only Europeans have the self-confidence to get away with this kind of verbal tennis.

'Oooo,' said Laurence, looking at me.

'How come you never let me talk to you like that?' asked John.

'I don't understand women,' said Barrie.

I'm ashamed to say I can't remember what the food was like because I fell asleep during which time the table of the people next to us collapsed and they all fell on the floor. Apparently, Sebastian gave them a look as if to say '*quel vulgarité*'.

I walked home through the black night and slid into the spa pool. Switching the pool lights off, I had nothing worse to listen to in the dead silence than the sound of the waterfall.

I jumped out of bed early, went for a walk, put the war-paint on and joined the others at the car park. Our first stop was the Boardwalk restaurant on the new Steamer Wharf and head chef Grant Jackson, whose stall had won the prize for best food in terms of decor, service, presentation and taste. Grant told me his great inspiration in terms of teachers was Dominique Parat, owner of GPK on Ponsonby Road with an old friend of mine Peter Howard, who has not yet forgiven me for not mentioning him in my first book, so I'm mentioning him now to get him off my back. Peter and I worked in the same restaurant in Paris for a period — two Peter(a)s and both New Zealanders in the same restaurant. I taught him everything he knows and then I also taught him to cook. He rewarded me by calling his restaurant in Sydney Rose Blues after mine in Paris. He is famous for his good looks, humour and even temperament. Opposites attract.

The Boardwalk cooks were the ones at the festival making the Crayfish (West Coast) *Bruschettas*. According to Marcella Hazan, real *bruschetta* is simply wholemeal bread slices grilled, rubbed or not with cut garlic and soaked in olive oil. The name *bruschetta* comes from *bruscare*, which means 'to roast over coals', the original and still the best way of toasting the bread. Each winter in ancient Rome, one's first taste of the freshly pressed, dense, green olive oil was most likely on a piece of *bruschetta*. In modern times, it became the staple of the poor man's *trattoria* and has now made its way into polite society, where it's the last word in deliciousness. Grant showed us how he makes crayfish and *bruschetta* fall in love with each other by keeping things simple and letting the delicate flavour of the crayfish stand alone on its merits. The crew were so enthralled with what I got to eat for the camera that Grant made them all crayfish sandwiches.

GRANT JACKSON'S CRAYFISH *BRUCHETTAS*

8 SLICES STALE BREAD

OLIVE OIL

8 RAW CRAYFISH MEDALLIONS OR THE TAIL OF A LARGE CRAY CUT INTO 1 cm *SLICES*

MIXTURE OF SALAD GREENS AND FRESH HERBS

1 RED ONION, FINELY SLICED IN ROUNDS

2 TOMATOES, DICED

HOME-MADE DILL MAYONNAISE

LEMON WEDGES FOR GARNISH

SALT AND FRESHLY GROUND BLACK PEPPER

Soak the bread in olive oil and grill lightly. Grill the crayfish for two minutes on both sides. Wash greens and herbs and toss together with the onion rings and diced tomato. To serve, arrange this salad mixture on the plates. Place the *bruschetta* in the centre with crayfish on top and dot here and there with mayonnaise. Garnish with lemon wedges, and sprinkle with salt and pepper.

DILL MAYONNAISE

CHOPPED FRESH DILL

2 EGG YOLKS

PINCH OF SALT

LITTLE LEMON JUICE

½ tsp DIJON MUSTARD

250 ml VEGETABLE OR OLIVE OIL OR A MIXTURE OF BROTH

In a round-bottomed medium-sized bowl beat or whisk together the egg yolks, salt, lemon juice and mustard. Add the oil drop by drop until the mayonnaise has taken, then gradually add it a little faster until it's a thin stream. Gently fold in the chopped dill.

On the way to my next adventure, Laurence and I stopped off for a *cappuccino* at Take Five, owned by Simon Hantler, who informed us it was the best coffee in Queenstown. On the counter were fat, heart-shaped shortbreads, with a stripe of chocolate, and freshly baked lemon-curd tarts. I asked Simon not to put too much froth on my *cappuccino*.

'Why not?' he asked.

'Because it messes up my lipstick and goes up my nose,' I replied.

'But, Peta, you're not supposed to sniff it.'

It tasted really good — strong, creamy, flavourful, thick. Simon absolutely knew how to make a *cappuccino* and he was terribly shy about his abilities along with it.

because I had a restaurant interview to do afterwards, I was dressed for parapenting in a visual symphony of synthetic ash-grey and lemon, three inches of makeup and jewellery, as is completely appropriate for the occasion. I had been talked into and was actually looking forward to sailing in a banana skin. What happens is you do it in tandem with an instructor — you sit in their lap for want of a better word, and sail away in the clouds. What the lovely Guy (my instructor) and Laurence had withheld from me was how you got from the gondola to the top of the mountain — you walk (climb would be a better word) up a steep cliff face for twenty minutes in your Romeo Gigli shoes. The gondola ride up the mountain was fantastic and Guy kept a perfectly straight face upon making visual contact with my get-up, being nothing if not amiable and relaxed.

We finally reached the summit. Guy was ahead of me despite the heavy parapent equipment he was carrying on his back. When I emerged from the pines, he was hiding behind his sunglasses and had his arms outstretched.

'Peta, you're going to kill me,' he said.

'You're right,' I replied, knowing immediately what was coming next. 'My clothes are soaked and I have to wear them all day, I'm enjoying heart palpitations, my legs are trembling and this goddamn makeup is melting' (and I'm not even nestled between your thighs, I thought).

'Look, I'm really sorry, Peta. The clouds you see over there are very dangerous and they've just come up.'

I was walking slowly towards him on the top of the mountain. He was on the phone to Laurence saying he needed help because I didn't look very friendly.

'Don't hit me,' he said.

'How could a cloud be so important, Guy?' I asked, hands on hips. 'Speak quickly and clearly.'

'You'd find out if you were in it. Honestly, I have to err on the conservative side, especially with people like you.'

'But you're not dealing with a conservative person here, and what do you mean by "people like you"?'

'Ha ha, I can see you're not conservative but what I meant was I have to be careful with TV presenters. How many people can you interview with broken legs?'

I sighed, turned around and tramped back down the hill, passing people on their way up wearing shorts, gym shoes and no makeup whatsoever. No sense of occasion. I smiled sweetly at them as I passed and didn't mention that there would be no flying that day.

You can't do a food show without wine, so off we drove to find some vineyards. The first one we came across was Chard Farm, clinging to the banks of the Kawarau River. It was established in 1987 by brothers Rob and Greg Hay. The view from the highway over the dramatic property nestled in right under the mountains, reminded Chris and me of Italian or southern French vineyards — rocky, dry and protected. Situated on a gentle slope, it looked like giant, odd-shaped handkerchiefs had been spread out on the ground.

They grow classic central European grape varieties — 'Chardonnay', 'Pinot Noir', 'Reisling', 'Sauvignon Blanc', 'Pinot Gris' and 'Gewürztraminer' — and are also trialing Méthode Champenoise and have run ice-wine trials when conditions have allowed. The Hays are so confident in the future of their cool-climate, elegant-yet-assertive wines they have invested with other developers in a large-scale grape-growing property overlooking Lake Hays.

The crew did some shots of the vineyard while I sat in the car scribbling and staying out of the sun. Chris returned with a large sprig of thyme for me, which spent the rest of the day in my hair, so I had to change my mind about beating him for the cliff-climbing episode. It reminded me of being in the Greek Islands years ago

when villagers gave me oregano and lemon thyme to put in my bag to scent it.

Our next stop was the famous Gibbston Valley French-look-alike winery located in the Kawarau Gorge, twenty-five kilometres from Queenstown, another vineyard that achieved a high profile very quickly. The driving force behind this venture is the dapper, bearded Alan Brady, general manager and developer.

When we turned up, Barrie said,'I remember this guy. I worked with him years ago for TV when he was a producer and he always had this dream for a vineyard, even then.'

Alan persisted in planting, firm in the belief that the climate with its hot, dry summers and cold winters had its parallel in overseas grape-growing areas. His optimism paid off, and his wines have received several New Zealand industry medals, and in 1994 the Gibbston Valley 1993 Chardonnay Southern Selection won a silver medal at the London International College wine awards. This is a small winery, but state of the art, and it has the capacity to produce 100,000 bottles, the main varieties being 'Pinot Noir', 'Reisling', 'Sauvignon Blanc', 'Pinot Gris' and a Southern selection made from Marlborough grapes.

I was left alone with Alan to sort out what we would talk about while the others filmed the vineyard. Within minutes, I was intimidated and unnerved by this man who was keeping me at arm's length and I was looking for a way out. Oh yes, I thought, I'll ask for a glass of the Pinot Gris that won the festival competition and talk about that — that'll chill him out. He got me a glass and declined to have one himself, which made me feel really, really comfortable.

'Alan, congratulations on winning the competition. Tell me about this wine,' I said, faking tranquillity by almost falling off the stool.

'Well, first of all it's not a big deal. Wine shouldn't be made for competitions, it should be made to enjoy — there are different views between the old and the new worlds. I feel we should be co-operating, not competing against one another. Quality equals taste, not medals,' he replied.

Did I get up and walk away? No. I ploughed on where others have feared to tread.

'OK then, so why has this Pinot Gris become a bit of a cult? Where do the grapes originate?' I asked.

'The grapes were originally grown in northern Europe in Alsace but have been grown in the Hawke's Bay for a long time, notably by Mission and Brookfield's. This particular wine is aromatic, complex, spicy and tastes of pears. We deliberately left in some sugar, and it has a good backbone of crisp acid. It will improve over two or three years, and we only bottled 200 cases.'

OK, OK, before I get thirty-seven letters saying how nice he really is, I'll tell you now that I did eventually find that out. It's the difference between the northern and the southern Irish. The difference between Protestants and Catholics.

The stylish 1994 Pinot Noir was there. Fresh and supple (according to the information on the wall) with good body and depth of ripe plummy, cherry flavour, this wine, having been fleshed out for a year in good quality French oak casks, should improve well into 1997 and beyond. Once I got into the new, flash caves and didn't want to come out, I tasted the four-month-old 1995 Pinot Noir from the barrel.

'"Pinot Noir" is really the grape of Central Otago,' said Alan, 'our vineyard is 45° south, the same as Bordeaux. I started in 1981 with half an acre as a hobby, and now I'm hosting 50,000 people a year at the winery and restaurant.'

These are the largest but not the most beautiful (they're in Blenheim but we'll get to that in the Marlborough chapter) caves in New Zealand. With the help of 1500 kilograms of explosives, over 1400 cubic metres of schist rock were excavated from the steep hillside behind the winery to form a tunnel leading to a complex of caves for barrel and bottle storage. They will eventually hold over

'HOW CAN I TAKE PHOTOS IF SHE WON'T BE SERIOUS!'

400 barrels mainly used for maturing Pinot Noir and Chardonnay with smaller quantities of Sauvignon Blanc.

The long, grey, concrete-covered caves provide a perfect haven for the maturing of wine. At a constant temperature of about 13.5°C, there is a harmonious interaction between the wine and the oak barrels. The floor was wet from seepage from the schist, and there was a window showing a view of 200-million-year-old, living schist rock. The quartz veins, glistening with gold, were formed by mineral aggregation in conditions of enormous heat and pressure when the rock was perhaps twenty kilometres below the earth's surface. It was divinely cool, and the more I cooled down, the more Alan warmed up. We got to talking about being Irish.

'The Protestant Irish are more dour and don't have the gift of the gab and the wildness of the Catholics,' Alan said with his soft Irish accent.

'I remember the flamboyant Irish friends of my childhood,' I confided, 'whose behaviour I found very permissive and down to earth in comparison to the strict household I was brought up in. Of course, I was madly in love with them and wanted to be with them twenty-four hours a day. They got drunk and the women talked about periods and sex and all sorts of outrageous things.'

'We quiet Irish would like to be like the extrovert Irish. We do try.'

What a charming man, I thought. He's turned from perfunctory to affable admirably quickly. Much as we abhorred the thought of going outside again, we eventually emerged to be hit by a wall of blue heat. After tea kindly arranged for us by Alan, we headed off for Clyde and the best accommodation of the entire series in terms of personalities, colour, warmth and comfort. What we didn't get out of people in interviews, we got out of Fleur around the dinner table in the evening.

Lake Wakatipu.

CHAPTER SIX

central otago

Convier quelqu'un, c'est se charger de son bonheur pendent tout le temps qu'il est sous notre toit — to invite someone, is to take responsibility for their happiness during the whole time they are under our roof

BRILLAT-SAVARIN

fleur Sullivan — the blonde bombshell. She's the best show in town; she's the only show in town. We drove from Gibbston Valley straight to Clyde, where Chris, Laurence, Barrie, John and I stayed with Fleur at Oliver's Lodge for three nights while filming our Central Otago episode. By this time it was becoming suspiciously obvious to me that South Islanders are more *sympathique* than North Islanders. The dictionary translation of *sympathique* is to get on well, to be sociable, to be nice, friendly, likable. It's the most accurate word I can come up with.

PETA AND FLEUR DISCUSS HAIRDOS.

'Don't be ridiculous, Peta,' scoffed my friends, 'South Islanders are dour, conservative and unimaginative.'

I didn't find this to be so. I'm sorry. I found out another thing of which I had not an inkling. Everybody else in the country has a low opinion of Aucklanders. They think they're all money, money, money, no soul, no culture, superficial high-flyers. What a joke. Can we help it if we have the most beautiful harbour in the world? Can we help it if the sun shines all the time (except when it's raining)? Can we help it that we're so good looking? Let's be mature about this — if anyone disagrees with me, I will stomp out of the room and slam the door.

But back to why I love the South Island. Fleur started off on a very good foot. When we straggled into her restaurant she exclaimed:

'Oh, you look beautiful. We need a bit of that around here.'

'Don't be too impressed,' I replied. 'Under this makeup is a tragedy.'

We arranged ourselves in our cool, large house. We had the whole place to ourselves with *en-suited* bedrooms, lounge and kitchen to do with as we pleased. While the others drank Speights on the lawn at stone tables, I went for a little evening walk around the village. What I found were lots of churches and lots of foxgloves. On my way back, I peered in a shop window and came face to face with Fleur, who invited me in to peruse her latest acquisition, the bank across the road. She's gradually doing it up to live in, and presently has her office there in a cocoon of maroon walls, velvet and antique lamps. Her wardrobe was full of Zambezi crushed velvet, cowboy boots with silver Harley Davidson tips, long silk scarves and things with sparkly things on them. Two of her friends/staff were in the kitchen eating chips from the restaurant.

'Oh, God!' they shrieked when I walked in, frantically shoving the paper in the rubbish, 'don't look at what we're eating. You'll be shocked. You're supposed to think we're the gourmets of the South.'

Fleur calls Clyde the Tuscany of New Zealand 'with its craggy hills softened with great sweeps of tussock grass and briar rose and banks of wild thyme tumbling over giant stacks of ancient stone ramparts'. The Oliver's complex was developed from the old main store, which had provided provisions for the goldminers of 1863. It is spread out over a block, comprising the big house, barn, deep cellars, stables, smokehouse and servants' quarters, with lovingly tended lawns and cobble-stoned courtyards joining everything. It's hard to describe the beauty and harmony of the place, but when you tell people you stayed at Oliver's they always smile and ask 'How's Fleur?' Everyone knows her, it seems, and they all feel she is their friend. Not one person I met in the food or wine business in Central (that's what you call it when you're on intimate terms) had a negative word to say about her or what she has done for the area. This is an incredible gift, all the more so because this woman is no wuss — she says what she thinks and uses four letter words, too.

SHOOTING THE FLEUR INTERVIEW.

That evening, we dined at the restaurant with its huge walk-in

fireplace, stone floors and high, green, wooden ceiling. The exterior is stone and dark green, covered with ivy. There's a grand piano, stained-glass lamps, paintings of naked ladies and antique dressers with a wide, wooden staircase going up to the bar. Spicy discussions at dinner as per usual, centring around food and

THE RESTAURANT AT OLIVER'S.

sex as per usual. We talked about man/ woman relationships and all agreed for once with my thesis that it is completely unrealistic to expect to understand the opposite sex.

'I get on very well with my wife,' said Laurence, 'and I'm still madly in love with her. I just remember the two rules.'

'What two rules?' asked Barrie, a glimmer of hope in his eye.

'Don't you know about Laurence's rules?' I smiled.

'Rule number one is the woman is always right and rule number two is, if you think she is wrong refer to rule number one,' said Laurence.

'Look,' I suggested, 'the best you can hope for is a good translator and exceptional communication skills.'

'Christ!' they all screamed, falling about laughing. 'We want less bloody communicating. We're sick of hearing them communicate.'

We finally decided that the ideal is to give our partners cell phones and lock ourselves in another room with another cellphone.

'Peta, how come you're such an expert on men, anyway?' asked Barrie.

'I read a lot.'

'Why are you so awful about New Zealand men and so over the top about French men?'

'How much detail do you want?' I said.

'None. I'm going to eat my soup instead,' he replied.

'What do you think makes a man or woman a great Casanova?' asked Laurence.

'Oh, I don't know,' I sighed. 'Someone who makes sure the encounter is enriching and both parties are left feeling happy and without regret, whether it's for a day or for a lifetime. A good lover is basically a giver.'

A male friend in Auckland says a man who gets quickly bored with women and is always looking for a new conquest is not a woman lover. All woman lovers are married and have no fear of commitment. They like living with women.

We ordered a Giesen's Marlborough Pinot Noir 1994, which was lovely. John had an openness and intelligent interest in life that I found very endearing. We discussed how you tell a good wine, a good meal, a good woman.

'If it's not brown and doesn't have bubbles then it can't be a good wine,' he said with that Dunedin charm.

'Dearest, there is life after Speights,' I ventured.

'Oh, I'm just a walking untrained palate. I can't tell the difference,' he moaned.

'John, if you trust your taste buds and think about what you're eating or drinking, you will train yourself all on your own,' I said. 'You are your own best teacher.'

'Nah, you really think so?' he asked.

'Look, you didn't like that meal last week. You were hungry but you didn't eat it,' I said.

'But I don't know why I didn't like it,' he replied.

'If you thought about it you would, and gradually you would develop a palate simply with practice.'

Dinner was followed by an exuberant single-malt whisky-tasting session that involved Laphroaig, Lagavulin and Talisker and any other unpronounceable names we could get our hands on. Lagavulin won hands down.

We retired to our boudoirs. Mine was yellow with an ornate frieze festooned around the walls and a duvet cover in green and gold with flower and berry varieties labelled in Italian. There was a fireplace, soft towels, fresh flowers, fruit in a bowl and a comfortable bathroom.

A door surrounded by tiny pink roses led from my bedroom on to the *provençal*-style courtyard full of red, pink and white hollyhocks and herbs growing out of the spaces in the paving stones. There were tables and chairs, a huge walnut tree, a dovecote with pigeons in it and a backdrop of mountains embracing everything. If there is a paradise, it must surely look like this.

In the morning, I realised I hadn't gone to heaven and had to get up and work. Breakfast had been laid out for us in the large dining-room of our house on the long *provençal*-style table. This room had stone walls and wooden floors, baskets hanging from the ceiling, vases of tall flowers and an antique dresser full of crockery. On the table were ducks, baskets full of lavender and our breakfast. There was a church pew in one corner and paintings and sculptures done by Fleur's son. On the sideboard was a line-up of huge bowls of fresh berries, stewed prunes, stewed apricots, stewed rhubarb, yoghurt, honey and various cereals. We and any other guests staying in other buildings all ate at this table, trying desperately to be civil at such an ungodly hour (7 am). Some angel from heaven was passing around tea and freshly brewed coffee.

'Is there anything else you would like?' she asked.

'Speed, cocaine, steroids,' we replied.

'Actually, I was thinking of bacon and eggs or an omelette with field mushrooms, or something like that,' she smiled.

'Nah, we're cool. Really,' said John.

Summer finds the Central towns of Alexandra, Clyde and Cromwell awash with New Zealand's best apricots. The same climate that loves grapes, loves apricots. It also loves nectarines, cherries, peaches and plums. The hot summers and crisp, cold winters are related to the ring of mountains and high plateau country acting as a barrier against coastal, moisture-laden winds. These winds shed their water on the peaks before reaching inland, resulting in Central's distinction as being one of the driest areas in the country, hence its official classification as semi-desert. Alexandra, which stands astride the Clutha, has the cleanest, sweetest air in the world according to Ian Mair, proprietor of Stonehouse Orchard on Springvale Road.

Ian and his family have added value to their roadside stall by preserving the fruits of their labours, and in a backyard shed they bottle apricots, not in a sticky syrup but in brandy. Each of the many fruits in their orchard takes its turn on the home-spun production line — quince pickle, Kirsched cherries, pickled walnuts, fruit sauces, rum pots and spiced blackberry pickle. There were apricot halves drying in the sun on wire racks. They are the imperfect ones

DISCUSSING PICKLED WALNUTS
WITH IAN MAIR.

that can't be bottled and are slightly sulphured to keep them sterile. We went for a stroll in the orchard full of voluptuous, intensely leafy green trees with red stems and bright orange balls all over them. There were rows and rows of blackberries. Not many city slickers know this but blackberry vines have arms — long six-foot arms stretching out like feelers. These will be tied up to be next year's fruiting.

I noticed little boxes in the trees, and Ian explained they were to control the codling moth and wasps. He doesn't use any insecticides, the dear man. The product that everyone is crazy about except *moi* is the famous pickled walnuts. Many of Ian's walnuts come from Fleur's gardens, and the taste panel for all his new product ideas is strangely enough based at Oliver's restaurant. They say people are addicted to Ian's pickled walnuts. All I can say is — it takes all kinds. In case you want to know, to make pickled walnuts you pick green walnuts before their shells have started to grow, then soak them in brine for six days. Leave them to dry in fresh air till they become wrinkly, then pickle in spiced or malt vinegar for two years. Then throw out. No. Just kidding. Call me old-fashioned, but I just can't *bear* the idea of interfering with baby walnut foetuses. Laurence set up a little *mise en place* under an apricot tree for our interview. Ian spends all his time getting rid of old rubbish, and Laurence spent all his time bringing it back again for the rustic display. He had choreographed Whitestone cheeses, walnuts, sprigs of lavender, old milking jugs and all the pickles in a very artistic composition.

Strangely enough, pickled walnuts are very good with other things. They add complexity and depth to dishes without your really knowing why the dish tastes different. Fleur uses them in her famous bunny and bambi pie and Antony Worrall Thompson in his wonderful *Modern Bistro Cookery* makes them hold hands with black pudding. He won't mind my writing the recipe down here because he believes there is no such thing as copyright with recipes. When you read Escoffier's *Le Répertoire de la Cuisine* written in 1914, you realise there is nothing new.

BLACK PUDDING WITH PICKLED WALNUTS

8 THICK SLICES OF BLACK PUDDING

25 g BUTTER

2 SHALLOTS, FINELY CHOPPED

60 ml WALNUT OIL

30 ml CORN OIL

1 APPLE, PEELED AND DICED

4 PICKLED WALNUTS, DICED

4 tbsp CHOPPED PARSLEY

30 ml CIDER VINEGAR

SALT AND FRESHLY GROUND BLACK PEPPER

Sauté black pudding in butter for two minutes each side. Remove and set aside. In the same pan add the shallots and oils and cook until soft. Add apple, cook for another two minutes then add walnuts and parsley. Pour in the cider vinegar and amalgamate with the other ingredients. Season to taste. I think this mixture would be good poured on to a bed of fresh tagliatelle.

After filling ourselves with Ian's partner Mary's home-made blueberry muffins, we moved off to our next shoot — me making a salad in a boat on the shore of Lake Dunstan. Inevitably, I was dressed in a creation perfect for a dingy and obviously the shoot was not at some easy-access site. It was down a long, rough track covered in weeds, rocks and minor rivers, hidden from view of any semblance of civilisation, St John's ambulance or Catholic priest, which I thought was a bit stiff. I mean, I know I don't believe anymore, but if I was drowning I might suddenly get my faith back. What I think, however, is approximately thirty-seven on the crew's list of priorities. Always the little humorists, Barrie and John tried to convince me that I had to sail out into the middle of the lake so they could do a long shot, then they did a pantomime about who was supposed to have brought the oars, and where were the life-jackets,

etc. I looked at the chief in his uniform of polo shirt, shorts and Roman sandals; he studied the ground.

They sat me in this stupid boat that almost sailed away twice, the wind was suddenly up, the sun had gone and the flowers flew out of my hair as did the shape. The boat was leaking, I was supposed to get the gas stove going on top of it all and there was not one piece of salad that was less than a foot long.

The cost of the massive Clyde Dam project might have nearly brought the nation to its knees, but whatever you might now think about it, the new Lake Dunstan is quite simply beautiful. Laurence prepared the ingredients for the salad from local produce and we finally got it all together.

SALADE A LA DUNSTAN

A HANDFUL OF CROUTONS
OLIVE OIL
A HANDFUL OF FRESH WALNUTS STRAIGHT FROM THE TREE
2 FRESH APRICOTS, THINLY SLICED
A MIXTURE OF HERBS AND SALAD GREENS
BALSAMIC VINEGAR
A LEAKY DINGY

Quickly fry the croutons in lots of olive oil, then throw in the walnuts and apricots for a minute, just to warm them through. Toss everything, including the hot oil, over the washed salad greens and sprinkle on a bit of balsamic vinegar. Eat, in a dingy, with your hands.

On the way back up out of our difficult and quaint location, the TVNZ van and car got stuck in a minor gorge. The owner of the boat and his incompetent assistants almost made things worse with their help, but the vehicles were finally relieved of their attachment to nature. I was thrilled that the rest of the crew had now joined me in the creative driving department.

In the afternoon, the sun came out again and we visited Kevin Jackson's orchard above Cromwell. His old orchard, which grew some of the best apricots in the world, was drowned by the man-made Lake Dunstan. Although this affected Kevin terribly, it didn't drown his passion for growing apricots. The first orchards were offshoots of the market gardens that provided for the goldminers. When the railway arrived, orcharding expanded rapidly. Today, making a living from growing fruit has gone a long way past the honesty box at the gate. Last year, Kevin's orchard produced 400 tons of apricots, half of which were exported. His packing operation goes on right in front of the local buyer at the rear of the large roadside stall.

The orchards were a truly amazing sight; acres and acres of ochre-and-green V-shaped rows. The trees are cut to have only two main stems and are trained on to huge, galvanised steel, V-shaped stakes at either end of the row, joined by industrial-strength wire.

ANOTHER 'PRODUCTION MEETING'!

'E minor,' said Barrie.

'What?' I asked. He had his sound boom up against the wire.

'The wire is tuned to E minor.' I looked at Chris. He looked at his sandals.

'By the way,' I said to John, 'no more close-ups of me eating food and no more shooting in the midday sun. From now on I'm going to get difficult.'

'You ARE difficult. Now get your girl-person over here and do some noddies.'

Noddies are when you have to look like you're deeply fascinated by a non-existent conversation. When you see an interviewer on television nodding in response to an answer from an interviewee, the conversation is usually long over and the interviewee at home having a cup of tea. I'm hopeless at noddies and always laugh, even if the person has just said their house burned down.

I interviewed Kevin as we strolled along the Vs and called him John. Sometimes all the names blur. Sometimes I can't even remember where I am. Kevin was nervous (probably about being called John) and tucked his shirt in so many times I believe it was threadbare by the end of the shoot. He confided he never gets sick of apricots — his parents were orchardists, his grandparents were orchardists and his children are partners in his business. Apricots need a good frosty winter for their blossom to set, and the worst ones he grows (i.e., the most visually perfect but the least tasty) are sent to the United States. The best ones, the older, yellow-coloured 'Moreparks' take a lot of beating for sweetness and that real apricot taste. You have to know which ones to buy when you go into a fruit shop — look for the labels. The 'Valley Golds' that go to California are built for beauty, not for brains. Kevin is well liked in the trade, and every break he does a smoko round of the orchard in his minimoke, taking tea and biscuits to the pickers.

On our way back to Oliver's John made us all disembark for a shot he wanted to do. In Cromwell there is a gigantic, kitsch, fruit sculpture on the edge of town. John had this clever idea that he would set up the shot so it looked like I was holding the fruit in my hand. As I was standing there with my hand held out, a tramp walked up to me and put a coin in my palm saying, 'There you go darling, that should see you right for a while.'

that night we did some filming in the restaurant. Fleur and her 'girls' were all decked out in Zambezi clothes to keep up standards. It had turned into a Zambezi competition. It was amazing — here were all these gorgeous women in the middle of nowhere dressed in Doc Martens and silk, wearing red lipstick and tattoos. We all sat down to a big meal at ten o'clock. Barrie, who loves offal, ordered Poorman's Croustade, which he pronounced to be heavenly, it being a pastry box stuffed with kidneys, sweetbreads, brains, bacon and mushrooms in a port sauce. Laurence and Chris had salmon, and the rest of us ordered steak. The food was good and my steak would have been like butter had I received it as I ordered it — medium rare. It was top quality, but unfortunately well done. Chefs in New Zealand do have a major problem with cooking medium rare steaks and I can't quite understand why.

This meal was accompanied by rivers of great Otago wine and huge, unending buckets of gossip from the locals regarding anyone we might be likely to meet down there, including all their relatives twice removed. We got mail-order brides, wives choosing two successive husbands with the same name, people driving their motorbikes through plate-glass windows, people in unison putting their fingers down their throats at the mention of a certain wine writer, husbands and wives running off with each other's partners, sons of rich families running off with the butcher's wife . . . As I was listening to this, one of the protagonists walked in and straight up to our table. Gentle reader, my face was a mask of inscrutability. A mask. Everybody else studied the bones on their plates closely.

We got to talking about how men are not so good at multi-tasking as opposed to women who can do many things at once. Certain testosterone-poisoned members of the table groaned. Fleur signalled encouragement. I thrilled to my thesis about the corpus callosum that I had stolen from my friend Gail and jumped up on to the chair.

'What's the corpus whatever?' asked Fleur.

'Thank you for asking. As everybody knows, the brain has two hemispheres that have different functions,' I shouted to loud ruckus from the riff-raff. 'Now, watch my lips. Joining the two spheres is the corpus callosum, which is a white band of fibres. It allows us to bring to bear information from both sides to problem solve, achieve things and do more than one thing at a time.'

'Have another drink,' John offered, 'and get off the chair.'

'Go on,' the girls screamed, 'we want to know what happens.'

'It is A PHYSICAL FACT that the corpus callosum is 40 per cent smaller in men than it is in women and it gets smaller as they get older.'

'So what?' asked Barrie. 'What a load of old bollocks.'

'Have you ever wondered why men get more rigid with age? Diminishing corpus callosum. This is why men can't multi-task. I rest my case.'

PETA AND FLEUR AT OLIVER'S.

It was when I felt Barrie pouring water on my feet that I decided to descend from my perch. Why waste my time on Philistines? Support then came from a completely unexpected quarter. Chris rose to my aid with the voice of reason and intelligence.

'Actually,' he said quietly, 'that makes sense to me. I find that men are very good at focusing on one project and blocking everything else off.'

Every day I was at Fleur's, I asked for a needle and thread to mend my slip that kept ripping in exactly the same place. There didn't appear to be a needle and thread in the entire county. Hand-sewing seems to be a dying art. Finally, I pinned it up with tiny gold safety pins. One day about a month later, I received a little, old-fashioned sewing kit from Fleur in the post. No name, no note — just an envelope with the contents.

■

In the morning, I rose, breakfasted and draped myself in chartreuse and *diamantés* to watch Fleur's head chef Kevin prepare the award-winning bunny and bambi pie, otherwise known as Rabbit, Venison and Pickled Walnut Pie. On the kitchen wall the definition of ENTHUSIASM had been copied from a thesaurus: ardour, eagerness, frenzy, earnestness, excitement, fervour, interest, keenness, passion, relish (not pickled walnuts, I hope), warmth, vehemence, zeal, zest. The bunny pie was the sort of dish one might get served up in Burgundy on a cold winter's night with good, thick, country wine. Fleur invented it when she was looking for dishes that were typical of regional products yet would not be seasonal.

'People like consistency. They like to be able to come back a year later and still find their favourite dish on the menu,' she said. 'I wanted to create a truly New Zealand provincial restaurant and a cuisine that would draw visitors to Central. Now I've done that and it was bloody hard work, I'm ready to move on to something else. Any ideas?'

'You could become a writer,' I suggested.

'Been done,' she said.

'Pack your bag, go to Paris and take it from there. I'll eat my earrings if you don't find inspiration within five days,' I said.

'You're so extreme.'

'I can't help it. I have an Irish passport, an unlimited supply of red dye and my mission in life is to get people off their backsides.'

RABBIT, VENISON & PICKLED WALNUT PIE

FOR THE STOCK:

RABBIT BONES

1 ONION, 1 CARROT, 1 STICK OF CELERY AND 4 CLOVES OF GARLIC, CHOPPED

1 cup OF RED WINE

SALT AND PEPPER

FOR THE FILLING:

1 LARGE ONION, CHOPPED

2 CLOVES OF GARLIC, CRUSHED

3 SLICES OF SMOKED PORK BELLY (OR STREAKY BACON)

OLIVE OIL

750 g DICED RABBIT MEAT (SAVE THE BONES)

750 g DICED VENISON

2 tbsp FLOUR

1 tbsp SEEDED MUSTARD

1 tbsp TOMATO PUREE

1 tbsp CHOPPED FRESH THYME

2 tbsp CHOPPED PARSLEY

1 tbsp WORCESTERSHIRE SAUCE

80 g MUSHROOMS, WASHED AND HALVED

12 PICKLED WALNUTS, HALVED

SALT AND PEPPER

CONTINUED NEXT PAGE

FOR THE PIE CASE:
250 g FLAKY OR SHORT PASTRY
1 EGG YOLK
MILK

Make the stock by roasting the bones and vegetables in the oven till they begin to caramelise. This should take about half an hour. Then put them in a pot with the red wine, just cover with water and simmer for one and a half hours. Strain the liquid off, discard the solids and reduce by hard boiling to one cup. Season to taste.

Make the filling by sautéeing the onion, garlic and pork belly in a little olive oil. Add rabbit and venison and brown. Stir in the flour till it disappears, then add the stock, mustard, tomato purée, herbs and Worcestershire sauce. Cover and simmer gently for forty-five minutes. Add mushrooms, pickled walnuts and season with salt and freshly ground pepper.

What you bake the pie in is now up to you. Fleur suggested large muffin tins but you could also use ramekins, small pudding bowls or throw the whole lot in a large pie dish. Line the container with rolled-out pastry and fill with the pie mix. Place half a pickled walnut on top, then brush the edges of the pastry with a mixture of egg yolk and milk. Cover with pastry, brush with egg yolk and crimp the edges together. Make a hole in the top of the pie with a skewer and decorate with pastry leaves and pastry walnuts.

Heat the oven to 220°C and bake the pie for thirty minutes.

Fleur serves these pies with Quince Chutney, a curly endive salad sprinkled with fresh walnuts, thin slivers of apple, and walnut-oil dressing (which she makes herself from the walnut tree in the courtyard).

Quince is a lumpy, yellow, furry fruit originating in northern Iran. They are lovely trees, about four metres high and almost as wide, and have a gorgeous scent that is famous for permeating the whole house. Keeping some in the linen cupboard ensures your linen stays fragrant. Quinces have white or pale pink blossoms that look like old roses and the woolly bottomed leaves turn buttery yellow in the autumn. They have a short season and a long cooking time.

QUINCE CHUTNEY

6 *QUINCES WITH THE STEM AND LEAF STILL ON*
6 cups *WATER*
4 cups *SUGAR*
4 tbsp *VINEGAR*

Rub the down off the quinces and wash them. Cook them on a medium heat in the water until the flesh starts falling off. Remove stem, leaves and stones. Add the sugar and vinegar and simmer for a couple of hours until the mixture thickens and turns a beautiful ruby colour.

Ian at Stonehouse gave me some Blackberry Pickle and Quince Pickle to take home, which is so delicious I eat it by the spoonful straight from the jar.

For some people the answer to the problem of how to make money from fruit and vegetables lies in tourism. The Jones' orchard shop in Cromwell even appears in the New Zealand tourism brochures in Korea. The day before, John had approached Mrs Jones who bit his head off. We found out later she was a good friend of the bus driver who had been killed in the bus accident we had seen two days previously in Queenstown, and was very upset. The bus had failed to negotiate a turn, no one knew why, the driver steering it into a tree to avoid plunging down the gorge. We saw locals and the police helping people out the windows. Today Eletheria Jones was back to being a typical Greek — friendly, generous and hard working. Chris obviously has a way with Greeks because at the end of the shoot he emerged laden with dried papaya, cherries, grapes, apricots and smiles.

In the afternoon, we went on safari into the wilderness of Conroy's Gully on the outskirts of Alexandra to the heart of the Central Congo and the wild man of wine — the inimitable Verdun Burgess. We had come across Verdun and his partner Sue Edwards at the Queenstown wine festival. He was blond, furry and genial, wandering around in his thick socks and fur-lined sheepskin boots with a smile and a pipe hanging out of his mouth. Great pair of legs. She was equally friendly and casually dressed and introduced him to me as her toy boy ('We live in sin.') If I liked Sue on impact, she turned out to be absolutely brilliant on closer inspection. Their vineyard is called Black Ridge and is the southernmost vineyard in the world. This rocky ravine is one of the most unlikely places I have ever seen a winery, but then Sue and Verdun aren't ordinary sorts of folks. Verdun was a carpenter from Invercargill and Sue was a teacher from Auckland, and they liken their discovery of grapes to gold fever. The impossibility of it all was the challenge.

I asked him why on earth he thought he could make grapes (anything!) grow out of the craggy, black rocks I found myself standing on.

'Oh — bone pig-mulish stubbornness,' he replied with a huge smile, rolling his Rs like a true South Islander.

'Yep, that's the one,' agreed Sue with an equally huge smile.

'In my opinion, New Zealanders are good at lateral thinking — it seems to be a national characteristic. Take me. I love rocks and I've managed to make a living out of it. I grew grapes because nothing else would grow here.'

I interviewed Verdun in the vineyard, which was easier than I thought it would be as he instantly thought he was the director. Talk about shy! It was painful to watch. Chris remained saintly patient as usual. Laurence took millions of photographs as usual, swapping fancy filters all the time. I could see Sue sitting up in the house on the top of the hill. Believe me, you have to see this place to believe it. It's so dramatic you wonder where Wagner is.

'We had to rewrite all the rule books and nothing worked like it should,' said Verdun, 'but the grapes seem to love the struggle and our customers like the result.' Bulldozers had to shape and mould the rock to allow pockets of grapes to be planted, and posts had to be drilled into the ground. The soil only goes down 500 millimetres.

There are now fifteen acres of grapes established in blocks around the hillside, with a further six to be developed. No insecticides are used, and they spray three times a year for powdery and downy mildew. Where grapes cannot be planted, the rocks are left to the wild thyme and the rabbits. The problem of rabbits led to many gross rabbit stories and jokes from Verdun. He maintained he grabbed them running downhill and shot them in the guts, thus avoiding having to empty them. All you have to do is rip their backs off. Sue laughed her head off at these stories. An acquaintance who grows organic grapes in Napier later told me how he cures his rabbit problem. First you get a gun-dog that will chase rabbits. He has a German short-haired pointer that has more qualities than the average dog — it can read. But, anyway, once the dog's killed a bunny you put a string around its neck (not the dog's) and hang it up on the post at the end of the vine. No smells, no blood. As it rots and dries, the other rabbits don't come near. That no other animal or human would either is an advantage or disadvantage depending on how much you depend on company. You can also put a plastic guard around the vine.

After the shoot, Verdun invited us up to the house for a 'cup of tea'. We got out of there three hours later and never even saw anything that resembled tea. We sat in a semi-circle in the bay window looking out on the orchards on the Earnscleugh Flats, gravel tailings from the gold dredging days and the Clutha River flowing through arid hills, dotted with poplars and willows. As the sun sank slowly in the west . . .

The first wine we were offered to taste was the Gewürztraminer 1995, the Black Ridge flagship. Bone dry and intense, it convinced me I can now drink this wine, for which I have only recently developed a taste. It's a soft wine with a broad palate showing good spice and pepper characteristics. I asked for some water. Verdun looked at me as if I were mad.

'Whatever for?' asked Sue askance.

'Calm down, sweetie, I meant water to swill the glasses out with,' I reassured her.

The next wine we tried was the off/dry Reisling with its classic lime and floral characteristics. I asked for the direction of the toilet and was told to be sure I opened the window and closed the door. Upon entering the bathroom I found a fixed window and a see-through door. In the other room, the assembled mass were falling about with the unbearable humour of it.

All the wines are aged in French oak. The barrels normally last four years, then they are sent to the cooper to be shaved and reburned, enabling them to last another three years. We moved on to the subtle, oaky Chardonnay, which, like the other two wines, wouldn't be released till October. Passionate, compelling, non-stop conversation flowed, Sue showing herself to be a wonderful, funny, intelligent woman completely without artifice. More water, then

Verdun cracked the Pinot Noir 1995, which really shouldn't have been touched for at least another year so we touched it anyway. Sue said wines in New Zealand are drunk far too young but are put on the market a year early purely for economic reasons. A year costs a million dollars. The Pinot was deliciously loaded with berries and cherry plums and toasty, toasty, toasty. It can be put down for up to ten years, which is what I intended to do when I bought it. Fat chance. It lasted as far as Napier two days later.

VINES AT BLACK RIDGE.

Finally, Verdun weakened and went down to get what I'd been patiently waiting for — THE (stand back) BOLLY OF BLACK RIDGE — THE AWARD-WINNING CHARDONNAY SELECT. He was also carrying a secret, unlabelled bottle. Well, it was too young but buttery, vanillery and very complex with only 0.3 grams of residual sugar. It had malalactic fermentation in oak then was aged on lees for nine months prior to release. Winemakers love nothing better than being asked questions about the process, and Verdun and Sue are no exception, in fact, Sue seems to be the only woman Verdun allows to speak. Getting a word in edgewise was the challenge of the afternoon. I guessed the contents of an unlabelled bottle as a Sauvignon Blanc. Verdun doesn't like it, so it won't be sold, but it was a good try.

It was dinner time but still light out as we reluctantly made moves to depart. One quick cup of tea later . . .

We drove carefully to Alexandra to dine in a restaurant Sue had recommended. When John saw the fish and chip shop, he slammed to a stop and refused to budge. Fifteen fish-chip-and-hamburger-laden minutes later, the five of us were squeezed on to a park bench on the river's edge, taking turns pushing the ones on the edges off. Unmitigated silence for a while then,

'Aren't the clouds beautiful,' I mused, 'what are they called?'

'Well,' replied John thoughtfully, pointing to them one by one, 'that one's Bruce, that one's George, and I can't see Fluffy anywhere.'

'Thank God for some decent food for a change,' said Barrie.

'Did your teacher really snap the pricks off rose stems to whack you with?' asked John out of the blue.

'Sure did,' I replied, 'and, as you can see, it didn't do me any good at all. I'm still sitting on park benches with a bunch of pricks.'

HOKIANGA HARBOUR.

CHAPTER SEVEN

hokianga and dargaville

a destinée des nations dépend de la maniere dont elles se nourissent —
fate of nations depends on the way in ch they feed themselves

the Hokianga's an interesting area because you can't get a good sit-down meal there but it has an ancient and dramatic history, is breathtakingly beautiful and relatively untouched by humankind. The beaches have white sand and blue water and the forest houses the largest kauri in New Zealand. The Hokianga Harbour saw the first Māori arrival (Kupe's canoe lies buried deep in a cave on North Head) and the Treaty of Waitangi was signed a second time there.

The glories and sorrows of war and love were the cornerstones of Māori culture, poetry and morality. The Māori was bred for battle, as the first Europeans discovered. The Pākehā was a combination of pet, mascot, slave, adviser and trader. Most of the original traders married chief's daughters, in fact, it was safer to do so, and a Pākehā trader in the family was of great value in terms of purchasing muskets, axes, blankets, pork and potatoes. By 1826 the Hokianga under the chieftainship of the powerful Horeke Patuone was incredibly prosperous. Colossal harvest feasts were held at Pakanae, where thousands of visitors would be invited to eat hundreds of tons of potatoes, kūmara, pork and seafood over a few weeks.

When reading up on the history of the Hokianga, I became entranced by the stories of relationships between Māori women and Pākehā men. In 1834 an Edward Markham lost his heart to a chief's daughter. 'She lived with him, hunted with him, dressed her hair with pigeon fat Parisian style, never left him, washed from head to foot with soap each night, killed the dog's fleas, knew all the Church prayers by heart, played a good game of draughts and swam like a fish. She saved his life when she brought him pistols in a brawl and attacked his assailant with a tomahawk. He had to return to England and their final embrace was tearful and bloody. She had gashed her whole body with oyster shells, a traditional expression of grief.'

It was wild territory, with the first Pākehā settlers being sometimes arrogant, cunning and violent men who believed in themselves to the point of megalomania. The Hokianga went into a gentle decline till the 1880s, when the wholesale slaughter of the inland kauri forest began, then in the early 1900s it was one of New Zealand's better dairy farming regions. The Hokianga Co-operative Dairy Company closed in 1958, which proved disastrous, and dairy farming collapsed over the next decade or two. People drifted south as they had been doing for a long time, resulting in the high unemployment and poverty now associated with the area. But the beauty remains, and it is one of my favourite areas of New Zealand because of the pervasive feeling of the drastic and intense history one experiences while there.

When Chris asked me if I had any leads on interesting food things happening in the Hokianga, I immediately thought of fish and chips and poetry. If food and sensuality go together, surely they can only be enhanced by poetry. In fact, I would like to know if Sam Hunt has yet approached the subject of this time-honoured staple of

New Zealand food. As part of my cultural experience every time I visit the Hokianga, I know that I have to buy some fish and chips. Why should I fight it? Who am I to laugh in the face of gastronomic folklore? Everyone knows the best fish and chips are to be found in Northland, until recently at Mangonui.

Last year I made a pilgrimage back to this holy Mecca to bow to the famous shrine, following up a visit from the year before. My friend and I had partaken of the feast on the verandah of the lovely old Mangonui Hotel overlooking the harbour — fresh snapper, perfect chips and Méthode out of plastic cups. You know how it is when you occasionally experience

LOOKING ACROSS THE HARBOUR ENTRANCE.

oneness with the universe. You know that this is it, you could not possibly be happier, THIS IS IT.

But when I arrived at Mecca last year after a journey through the wilderness, my eyes fell upon a sight so horrifying, it was almost more than flesh and blood could bear. The fish shop had been discovered and bought by folks who clearly had ideas about themselves. In place of the little, incompetent, down home, friendly place I remembered was a shiny, clean monstrosity with numbers you had to take and seating. SEATING for God's sake. The staff wore uniforms. UNIFORMS for God's sake. Where was the nice lady in jandals and grubby apron? Where were the big fat wedges of lemon?

My friend Davina who used to live in the Hokianga, told me the fish shop at Omapere (A mau Purrie) would not trifle with my emotions. I went straight to this shop and bravely swung aside the plastic fly curtain. Zero decor, menu on blackboard on wall, reek of cooking oil and poor ventilation, insufferably hot, small, no uniforms. So far so good, but I was not so foolish as to be lulled into a false sense of security. Outside was a line-up of Harleys and Ducatis and on the porch were members of the public cleverly disguised as torture chambers — compositions of chain mail, rawhide, tattoos and areas of free space once occupied by denim. Tangata whenua from somewhere down the line were there for lunch. The most impressive of them was a mountainous factory of a man, for whom the word obese had long ceased to be appropriate. On the table in front of him was spread about thirty-seven kilos of fish and chips.

'Where's the fuckin' bread?' roared the factory. Buttered slices of white bread arrived piled a foot high. This was a person whose ancestors arrived in the very treacherous harbour facing us in the fourteenth century. This was a person whose ancestors enjoyed cannibalism. This was a person whose land is of enormous spiritual significance. I say if the man wants bread, give the man bread. I placed my pathetic little order and returned an hour later when I had seen the procession of bikes pass Davina's house. The fish was just sliding into the vat from Bruce's capable hands, and a conversation ensued. My background had been established through Davina. Bruce was Pākehā, bearded, tattooed — a poet of some repute, a charmer, a storyteller. A man who writes for social change and revolution from within.

He told me the story of a gentleman who had turned up at closing time asking how many chips he could get for forty dollars. He and his extended family had been on the marae for three days and were desperate for a feed of Pākehā food. They ended up spending $150. Bruce's wife Jan was the sort of woman I always want to follow home and ask if she will be my mother. She had a beautiful, unlined, intelligent, happy face framed by hair that reached to her tailbone. Upon receiving my treasure I made a hole in the newsprint to expose the fresh snapper in light batter, fat chips fried to perfection in clean soya oil and wedges of lemon. Bruce filleted the fish himself and they just leapt straight out of the harbour into his shop.

I experienced oneness with the you-know-what.

This year I was accompanied by the crew of Chris, Laurence,

cameraman Alan and soundman Richard from Auckland. Bruce was full of tall stories and short shrift and spouting poetry at the drop of a chip as usual — it was a pleasure seeing him again. The shop was the same and there were 1971 magazines on the table for the punters to peruse. I was particularly attracted to the hairdos. Bruce had arranged for a mate to turn up with some horses in case I could be talked into getting up on one. The idea was I had to buy some chips, get on my trusty mare and ride away into the sunset. Obviously, I was wearing a pale-pink shirt that was filthy within seconds of looking at the animal. Horse was twice my height and it was so high I couldn't even get my foot in the stirrup, but eventually with a hand up from Hewie, the owner of the horses, I found myself facing the right way and quite liking it. I like the smell of horses.

'Ya gotta be careful with women who don't know how to ride horses,' drawled Hewie to me, 'you've always got to make it look like it's not your fault.'

'Yeah right. You and three million other men,' I replied.

'Don't be like that,' said Clint Eastwood (Hewie's surname was actually Eastwood).

'Hewie, can I share something with you?' I said. 'I actually have

ALAN HOUGH GETS A CLOSE-UP SHOT OF BRUCE'S FRIED FISH.

never ridden a horse before. How do you steer it? How do you start the ignition?'

'Christ! I thought you knew.'

'How would I know? I'm just a simple cook.'

It didn't matter what I did, I couldn't get the thing to start, so Hewie had to lead the horse by the reins. Then Chris decided to do some beach shots with me casually riding across the scene.

'Now, Peta,' he said, '*if it's possible* could you ride down this little rise over to that rubbish tin. *If you can.*'

Chiquita (the horse), of course, cantered. I was thrilled to within an inch of myself that I was still upright, so of course Chris said, 'Could you do that again but no jig-jogging this time. No looking as if you're out of control.'

Out of control! Excuse me, but I was practically National Velvet out there. Cantering not jig-jogging, thank you. In my opinion, I had been impressive without necessarily inspiring *absolute* confidence, but out of control I was not.

Hewie confided in me the secret of his happy life — 'No wife, no kids, no worries.' It was simple but it was deep.

Every day except Monday Bruce puts on his fish and chip show, a dinner wrapped in the best Northland newspaper, which he reckons can't be beaten anywhere. The man's no charlatan. He once fished the seas for a living, but finds life as a storyteller, poet and fish-and-chip shop man a better way of life. Life in the Hokianga has always been taken at an unhurried, leisurely pace just the way the locals like it. Some locals, seriously under the influence of the major cash crop in these parts, were supposed to have been rounded up by Bruce to be customers for the shoot, but they never turned up.

'They like *watching* TV,' said Bruce, cracking a big smile, 'but they don't like being on it.'

We found out the next day that they turned up that evening for the afternoon shoot, asking for the TV man.

'Don't they know what 5.30 means?' I asked Bruce.

'Depends what kind of 5.30. Hokianga time or world time. They will have sat around all afternoon getting dakked up for the big event. No point in rushing things.'

This concept is very similar to Greek time. You ask what time the next bus is coming and they say, 'After the next cigarette.' We watched some people getting out of their car outside the fish shop.

'It's easy to tell non-locals,' sneered Bruce, 'they check their hair before getting out of the car, then they lock the car, then they double-check it. Locals look on the polite side of casual to put it mildly and no one can remember the last time they saw a car with a lock on it.'

Here is one of Bruce's poems.

STICKY WORD PLAY POEM

As I went walking out one morn
I spied a most peculiar chap
Sticking stucco on a wall
His trowel went flap flap flap.

And then from out of nowhere came
A bandit naughty
Proud and haughty
Levelled his gun straight at
The contents of our noble plasterer's hat.

'Stand and deliver' he then did order
'Your lunchbox or your life!'
I ran up closer just to help
The plasterer from his strife.

I plucked my own gun from its holster
And yelled with neither stay nor stutter . . .

'Stick 'em up you stucco sticker upper sticker upper.'

As is standard for all our shoots, the hospitality was exemplary. Coffee was served and a special iced sponge cake had been made by the daughters. We were lodged up the road, so decided to take our evening meal there, having already feasted on fish and chips for lunch.

I was told that John Cleese got his inspiration for *Fawlty Towers* from a hotel in Torquay. This is clearly untrue as the inspiration obviously came from the place we stayed at. It would have been entertaining had they been rude or hostile, but they didn't even have the grace or personality for that. The service was partially done by ourselves, for example, procuring water, glasses, tables, serviettes, and partially by begging the waitress and proprietor numerous times for simple necessities such as food and wine. As there were only

1995 wines on the list, Alan asked if there might be any other more ancient vintages lying around somewhere. Basil returned with a decrepit 1988 Sauvignon Blanc. We blanched. Would he mind awfully having another look? This time he came back with some Houghton's white Burgundy 1994, which Alan decided to chance. It turned out to be a cheapie but a goody that didn't disappoint, I believe. We arrived at 8.15 pm and dinner was finally served at 9.45 pm.

If the service was appalling, we hadn't yet tasted the food. I won't even discuss it except to record that if in some moment of delirium I thought I was going to get a medium-rare steak, it had obviously been in a state of pre-diabetic euphoria. Hunger will provide hope where no hope could possibly flourish. Witness making a bad marriage for example – people are driven to marry by hope and emotional starvation. But the really halucinogenic thing was that, unlike *Fawlty Towers*, the other members of the crew, when asked by Basil how things were, all smiled in unison and chirped:

'Fine thank you. Everything's great.'

I stared at them. To have a waiter who was a walking anthology of bad service, a serial offender no doubt, actually adding insult to injury by asking if everything was all right was more than my, by now, limited resources could cope with.

Alan leaned towards me and said sympathetically, 'You're reaching your limit aren't you?'

'I'm afraid I am and what makes it worse is you're all lying your heads off. It's quite obviously not all right and you're all telling them that it is. Why are you engaging in this criminal activity?' I simpered, ripping my napkin to shreds.

'We can't be bothered telling the truth,' said Laurence. 'We don't want a fuss.'

'Don't want a fuss' is the major cause of coronary occlusion in this country.

'But, dearest,' I said, 'you've owned a restaurant and so have I. If I owned a restaurant I would want to know if things were bad.'

'You assume he doesn't know.'

'Can't be bothered,' they all chorused.

'But Basil and Sybil are not only making a fool of you, they are asking you to pay for it,' I pleaded.

'It's true really,' piped up Chris. 'It's even too dodgy for me. The vegetables are all frozen (frozen carrots?) and my fish is rigid.'

'A distinct lack of the kūmara we were promised,' said Laurence nicely to Sybil.

'Oh,' said she, 'my silly husband didn't peel enough and the Rotarians over there at that big table were given too many.'

By this stage, Alan was allowing himself to get a bit tetchy. I was looking around at the other tables wondering if it was just us, when a woman leaned over with a sardonic smile and asked,

'Enjoying Basil and Sybil? Aren't they unbelievable?'

Our mission the next day, should we choose to accept it, was to catch fish in the Hokianga Harbour. I left the crew sitting in the restaurant and sloped off to my huge dwelling overflowing with single beds and crickets that jumped on my reclining person. Everyone was kept awake all night by screaming cats.

at the crack of dawn we were to be found trail-blazing on the bracing deck of the ferry to Rawene (the place of the rising and setting sun), admiring the stunningly clear unveiling of the new day. The mist was rising off the land like steam off a spinach soufflé. When we reached Malcolm and Betty Pinkney's dock, they were already out on the harbour having put their nets down earlier. They

THE CREW ALL VIE FOR SPACE ON MALCOLM'S BOAT.

fish about nineteen days a month when the tides are lowest, otherwise there's too much rubbish. Twenty-five years ago, Malcolm and Betty gave up their fast-lane life in Auckland and came to the Hokianga to build boats and go fishing. Twin boats, twin people. Betty had her fringed hair in a ponytail and wore a sweatshirt with green rubber overalls, and Malcolm wore a check shirt with green overalls and an oilskin hat. They were a picture of health and heartiness. His hand-made boats are a traditional Scandinavian design with both ends fairly blunt to enable easy wave riding.

They were the most beautiful boats — bleached, clean and tenderly aesthetic. There was an acute line-up of anchors, a winch and a carved shovel for the ice.

I jumped on Malcolm's boat and the crew jumped on Betty's.

'Where's your gear?' asked Malcolm. 'You can't go fishing in that outfit.'

'They make me do it,' I replied. 'They tell me we're going to film a fishing boat but they don't tell me I'm the one who's going to be fishing.' A conversation ensued about all the awful things they make me do. We motored out to the nets and Malcolm drew them in. Not a huge catch but better than a poke in the eye with a burnt stick. Ninety per cent of the catch was flounder, which was gutted immediately and placed in a box full of ice. It's essential to ice fish the minute it is caught — every hour it is out of ice shortens its shelf life by a day. There was this life-and-death chain happening right before our eyes. It's Malcolm's fish that find their way to the Omapere Fish and Chip Shop and he's very careful about how he looks after them. There was no fish smell in the boat whatsoever, which made me realise how old the fish must be that is sold in some fish shops in the cities. My TVNZ bag that I carry everywhere containing makeup, knives and notebook was too close to the enthusiastic gutting procedure and got splattered in viscera. Not only did this look really attractive but it smelt really good by the end of the day, too.

That night I put my foot down about the dining arrangements, and as Malcolm had given us his catch of flounder, we decided to have a barbie in the grounds of the motel. Laurence fried kūmara on the barbecue, I made some salads, Alan took the wine selection under control and Chris did the dishes. The fish was desperately good, and it was probably one of the best meals we had in the whole series. It rained, but we were so delirious at getting a good meal that we sat there and laughed all evening, solved a few world problems, listed the names of people we would never marry, and went to bed to listen to what sounded like a fight between wild tigers and boars all night.

On the way to Dargaville through the Waipoua Forest, we stopped off at the Panorama Tearooms. This monument to bad taste was in the most fabulous situation with a million-dollar view of the Hokianga Harbour. No decor to speak of, save plant holders that looked like Stevie Wonder's hairdo, synthetic curtains, railway cups and saucers, aluminium teapots and tea bags. This was no Epicurean eatery, but I have to say I couldn't complain about paying $1.50 for a cup of tea and an unbelievable vista.

We drove through the remnant of what were once vast Waipoua kauri forests. As late as the early 1970s, hundreds of hectares of kauri were ruthlessly milled in Warawara Forest. We paid homage to Te Matua Ngahere — the biggest tree — looking up at the canopy and down at our feet as we walked along the track. The sign said 'You are in the heart of a small remnant of one of earth's most ancient ecosystems. Breathe deeply and tread softly.' Pity we had to end up in Dargaville at the end of it, but the chief said kūmara so kūmara we were off to do.

TALKING TO ANDRE ABOUT KŪMARA.

The next scene found us all knee-deep in the silty, dusty, clay soil of a kūmara field near the Wairoa River. The minute you walk on this earth, you are covered in it, so naturally I was asked to sit in it. The upside was I got to sit in it with André de Bruin, a tall, dark, good-looking man with very white teeth. I know what you're thinking — good research department, but I swear it was just a stroke of fate. Alan was doing a wide 'non sync two shot crossed with a long back shot' (I just put that in to impress you) wherein André and I had to look at each other. He was supposed to talk and I was supposed to keep my mouth shut, always a difficult situation but in this case it was absolutely no problem for me — I could have looked at him all day. André is a horticulturist who for some reason just loves talking about kūmara. It was impossible to get him to be brief because his knowledge and love of his job just spilled over. When Chris asked him to say it all again in one sentence, André just smiled and started all over again on the complicated story of kūmara.

Kūmara is not a type of potato, thank you very much. It doesn't even belong to the same family. It's a tuber and a tropical plant brought to New Zealand in Kupe's canoe, but originally from South America. The fact that it grows in New Zealand at all is miraculous, it being finicky, prone to disease and easily damaged or broken. It doesn't grow down under the ground like a potato — it is planted on an angle in shallow, built-up rows. The kūmara are found just beneath the earth sprouting off sort of vines that traverse the top of the soil. The Māori originally planted and harvested in back-breaking but very ritualistic, hand-hoed style.

Kūmara harvesting.

Incredibly skilled gardeners, they developed sophisticated horticultural knowledge, including caterpillar control by the use of tame black-backed seagulls, exploitation of the climate and clever storage pits. These days the tuber is planted and harvested by machine. Kūmara hate frost and they have to have a long, hot growing season with warm nights and sufficient moisture. The soil has to be new and clean with no leftovers from last year, and the tubers absolutely have to be harvested before the winter rains. It's all terribly nerve-racking.

Having rolled around in the dust for quite long enough, we moved on to the big Delta Produce sheds in town to film the processing, curing and packing of kūmara. Basically, the kūmara is a fresh product and should, ideally, be consumed as such. Never put them in your fridge. If you will persist in being perverse and not eating them as soon as you buy them, wrap them in newspaper or bury them in dry sand or sawdust and they will last up to six months. Unfortunately, the man who was supposed to be bringing in truckloads of kūmara from the fields for the shoot didn't turn up because his wife had chosen that very moment to go into labour. Glen of Delta offered me a shirt emblazoned with his logo, making it clear I was expected to wear it for the kūmara-cooking segment.

'Get real,' I said, 'I have chosen this hand-painted silk bit of frippery for my cooking class.'

'OK, Petra, that's fine,' he replied, 'well . . . here's the shirt anyway. It's for you.'

'Thank you, Glen,' I said sweetly, thinking of the gym.

'Why don't you want to wear the shirt, Petra?' asked Alan.

'You call me Petra one more time . . .'

'The *Listener* says it's Petra.'

'The *Listener* has given me three different names so far, and if silk is all right for getting down on my hands and knees to grovel in kūmara fields then it's all right for cooking.'

We were invited out to lunch at the Central Hotel. This was the menu:

> Sirloin steak $8.50
> Ham steak $7.50
> Fish Tartare $7.00
> Chicken nibbles (can't remember the price)
> Above served with salad and chips
> Egg .50c

No person in any language could possibly argue with the prices. The salad and chips were delicious. There was a jukebox, a pool table and plastic plants — things were looking good. I ordered a Guinness and a medium-rare steak. Laurence asked me why I wished to make a victim of myself.

'But I've given the waitress explicit instructions as to the construction, method and Latin origin of the words medium rare,' I said confidently. 'I feel sure I will see blood. It will be fine.'

And it would have been if I had ordered well done.

Well, if you thought the kūmara patch was boring, the afternoon found us in John Smith's kitchen on River Road trying to make silk purses out of sow's ears. Every year, Dargaville hosts a kūmara festival. The brief was to interview Alvin, winner of the kūmara-cooking competition and demonstrate my Brazilian sweet potato mousse. Alvin was a mass of nerve endings looking for a big dark hole.

'So, Alan,' I asked, 'why do you like kūmara?'

'Alvin.'

'I beg your pardon?'

'My name's Alvin.'

Shrieks of laughter from *moi*. Nervous tick from Alvin.

'So, Alvin, why do you like kūmara?'

'Don't like them much at all, except maybe roasted sometimes.'

'So, Alvin, why did you enter this competition?'

'Something to do.'

'Alvin, can I share something with you?' I whispered, 'Don't give me these answers when the camera's rolling OK?'

'I know I'll never get it right,' he smiled sheepishly, 'this is a terrible day. The worst day of my life. I was fine till you guys turned up.'

The entire shoot was filmed with Pearl Harbour Two going on outside. There was an air show on and every time I got Alvin to say more than one syllable a plane roared overhead. He was trying really hard to talk, but his answers were given with the lack of enthusiasm that can only come from one who deeply despises kūmara. In spite of this Alvin had created a truly wonderful pie for which many viewers wanted the recipe.

With this crew, I had three people saying GO in three different ways. First Chris said 'roll', then Alan said 'very ready', then Richard said 'speed'. I hadn't a clue when to start so did nothing till everybody stopped saying

'SO, ALVIN, WHY DO YOU LIKE KŪMARA?'

things. At one point, I was making my mousse and prattling to the camera when Alan turned around and looked out the window, so I stopped talking. Wrong. If the cameraman goes for a walk while filming, it is none of your business. I have to say, though, that Alan and Richard were gorgeous to work with — always the sardonic humour and friendly smiles. This is Alvin's prize-winning cheesecake:

ALVIN'S KŪMARA & LIME CHEESECAKE

FOR THE FILLING:
750 g PEELED KŪMARA
¼ tsp CHICKEN STOCK TO COOK THE KŪMARA IN
1 tbsp GELATINE
4 tbsp WATER
250 g CREAM CHEESE
JUICE OF *6* LIMES
1 can CONDENSED MILK
¼ cup SOUR CREAM
2 EGGS

Cook kūmara in water and chicken stock till very soft. Drain. Mix the gelatine in the cold water and stand for ten minutes. Place the cooked kūmara in the blender with the cream cheese, lime juice, condensed milk, sour cream and eggs and process until really smooth. Add the softened gelatine.

FOR THE BASE:
2 pkts OF BISCUITS (LIKE WINE BISCUITS)
150 g MELTED BUTTER
27 cm SPRING CAKE TIN

Crush the biscuits till very fine then add the butter. Press the mixture into the base and sides of the tin.

Pour in the cheesecake mixture and refrigerate for at least six hours or overnight. Decorate with chocolate flakes and semi-circles of finely sliced limes all around the edge.

This next recipe is from my restaurant in Paris. I had a lot of Brazilian friends and they taught me how to dance, how to be generous and how to cook their dishes. All Brazilian desserts have enough sugar in them to account for the sweetness and sensuousness of the entire nation, but as there is no passion in New Zealand, I have halved the sugar content to make the mousse palatable. It is completely addictive.

MOUSSE DE BATATA DOCE

FOR THE MOUSSE:
500 g KŪMARA, PEELED
90 g BUTTER, SOFTENED
100 g SUGAR
1 tsp VANILLA OR HALF THE CONTENTS OF A VANILLA POD SCOOPED OUT
1 EGG YOLK

Cook the kūmara without salt until very soft. Drain. In a blender process the cooked kūmara with the other ingredients till very smooth. Spoon the mousse into small ramekins or one serving bowl.

FOR THE CHOCOLATE SAUCE:
100 g DARK COOKING CHOCOLATE
2 dessertspoons SUGAR
2 dessertspoons BUTTER
125 ml (1/2 cup) MILK

Melt the ingredients together and pour on top of the mousse. Refrigerate, serve cold with whipped cream and start dancing.

Dinner that night was at Lorna Doone restaurant. We had no choice in the matter — those were our orders and we couldn't be bothered arguing. Laurence and I drove to our fabulous motel, which was so bad Chris decided it was a national treasure and we should see it in that light. We sat in the car outside the office and presently I stopped putting lipstick on and noticed that Laurence was squinting intently at the swimming pool.

'What are you looking at?' I asked him.

'I'm trying to work out if it's a walrus or a seal,' he replied. We both peered. Suddenly the hairy lump raised its head and looked straight at us.

'God, Laurence!' I gasped. 'He heard you.'

'No he didn't. No he didn't.'

We both collapsed into small balls in the front seats.

Actually, we went to the restaurant to escape the orange, *single*, candlewick bedspreads, formica walls and fifties decor. Determined to make the best of things, we had brought our own wine and threw ourselves into it immediately as a sort of anaesthetic against what we feared was to come. All the signs were there — prawn cocktail, roast dinner, bad decor, lace tablecloths, etc. The food arrived a normal period of time after ordering and everyone made a point of not looking at me or encouraging me in any way. At the end of the meal, I pronounced that although the lamb was overcooked, the vegetables and sauces were delicious — honest, good, country fare. The Scottish lad in the kitchen obviously had a way with sautéed potatoes.

'Well, thank God for that,' said Chris.

We were so enamoured of the repast that we asked to see the chef to thank him, only to be told that for some unfathomable reason, he had sloped off home.

'Get him back,' we all shouted.

'But he's gone home to bed,' said the waitress.

'Get him out of it then. We want to meet him,' we screamed, thumping the table.

The spherical Peter came back, of course, which was when the evening really began. I sang a song, Laurence played the piano and we flung open the doors and windows, which up until then had remained closed despite the heat. It turned out to be the swan-song because the restaurant had been sold and that night was the last.

kumeu and
puhoi

tko dobro ije, bolje; a tko
vele pije, malo ije — who
eats well, drinks better; who drinks too
much, eats worse

the Dargaville and Kumeu shoots were done back to back, so it was on a rainy Sunday morning in February that we found ourselves driving from a land dominated by flatness of both geography and spirit to a land dominated by lushness of growth and character. There was no question the Yugoslavs were considered aliens when they first arrived in North Auckland. They drank, they worked inhumanly hard, they danced, they sang and they had a national propensity to hot bloodedness. It's a wonder we didn't lock them all up, but in the 1950s we did lay down a few laws to stop them having a bad influence on us. With a convoluted way of thinking that only governments have, they restricted sherry sales to two-gallon jars so we might be saved from undesirable drinking habits. Drinking Dally wine might have led to looseness and God only knew what might have happened then. This might seem laughable now, but no more so than our present restrictions on buying alcohol.

I remember the school dances when I was a teenager. The nuns at St Mary's College periodically arranged knees-ups with the brothers at St Paul's and Sacred Heart, and my friends and I preferred the Dally boys because they were better looking and better kissers than New Zealand boys. The next Monday at assembly 'certain girls on the fast road to hell' would be singled out for unladylike behaviour. We would raise our eyes heavenward and trudge off to Mother Benedict's office.

The TV shoot was to be hosted by Jordanka and Kruno Vitasovich of K.V. Wines in Kumeu at a spit roasting of lamb in the traditional way. Chris called ahead on the cellphone to ask if the spit was still happening as it was by now pouring with rain.

'Of course,' they roared, 'we've got sixty friends turning up for this. We'll arrange for the rain to stop.'

We were greeted by Jordanka, a tall, gentle, handsome woman who gave us complete run of her spotless home and property. Her husband Kruno, a tall, good-natured man who didn't speak a lot of English, follows the family tradition, making Dalmatian-style wines just like his uncles before him. For years the Dalmatians who brought their horticultural and winemaking skills with them were New Zealand's only winemakers, concocting country wines and syrupy sherries as only they knew how. The rain had reduced itself to a light drizzle as Kruno's friends busied themselves preparing the spit in the shed behind the winery. The vines were wearing their white veils and everyone was in a good mood.

While the crew wandered around setting up their shots, I got into a conversation with our 'guide' George Mihaljevich, president of the Dalmatian Culture Group. In between the racket and imbroglio of the cooking, he gave me a history lesson that was so complicated I lost track somewhere in the foothills of Austria. He patiently recounted that Dalmatia stretched along the Adriatic coast from Zadar down to Dubrovnik. It was under the kingdom of Venice when it was snatched in 1812 by Napoleon, who made it part of the kingdom of Illyria. The British then gave it to Austria and it became

LAMB ON THE SPIT, DALMATIAN STYLE.

the kingdom of Dalmatia. In 1918 after the First World War, Dalmatia became part of a kingdom of Serbs, Croats and Slovaks, which became known as Yugoslavia in 1929. In 1941 this was broken up under the Nazi occupation of World War II and in 1945 was reconstituted by Tito. He set up a federation of six republics, and Dalmatia was put into the Croatian republic. Dalmatia's long time under the Italians shows up strongly in terms of language, food and architecture.

This conversation took about an hour because we were constantly interrupted by people saying 'make sure you tell her about such-and-such' or 'that's not how it happened at all' or 'let George tell it, he has the knowledge' or 'eat this, Peta, eat this' or 'I want you to write down the story of my life'. George, who didn't appear to share any of the personality traits of his compatriots, smiled placidly, spoke softly and accommodated everybody. Millie offered us strong, sweet, Turkish-style coffee and *Fritule*, which are baby doughnuts with raisins in them, deep fried and swamped in sugar. Berta offered us some *Makarana* and gave me the recipe and some of her other favourites. All around us people were yelling their heads off in *Hrvatski*, the Croatian language. At first I thought they were arguing, then I understood that they just talk loud. In Yugoslav culture there are absolutely no Indians, only chiefs, and that goes for both men and women. Chris had to share his directorship with at least a dozen other people.

MAKARANA CAKE

BASE:
200 g/1 cup FLOUR
PINCH OF SALT
1 EGG
2 EGG YOLKS
2 tbsp SUGAR
2 tbsp BUTTER, MELTED

TOPPING:
5 EGGS
1½ CUPS SUGAR
1 tsp VANILLA
1 tsp RUM
¼ tsp LEMON ESSENCE
150 g GROUND ALMONDS
150 g WALNUTS, FINELY GROUND
1 tsp BAKING SODA

Base

Mix all the ingredients together in a mixing bowl until they form a dough-like mixture. Press three-quarters of the dough into a 25 cm cake pan lined with greased baking paper. The remaining quarter of dough is to be left for decoration.

Topping

Separate eggs. Beat egg yolks and sugar until thick. Mix in vanilla, rum and lemon essence. Add ground almonds, walnuts and baking soda. In a separate bowl beat egg whites until soft peaks form. Fold into egg-yolk mixture. Pour over prepared base. Decorate with strips of rolled pastry. Bake at 200°C for half an hour.

Serve with coffee.

DALMATIAN *PARADIŽOT*

1 pkt VANILLA WINE BISCUITS
1 l MILK
4 EGGS
4 EGG YOLKS
2 tbsp SUGAR
1 tsp VANILLA ESSENCE
1½ tbsp CORNFLOUR
2 tbsp MILK
1 tbsp GRATED CHOCOLATE

In a serving dish place the vanilla biscuits into a single layer. Dish should be flat with 75 mm sides. Bring milk to the boil in a saucepan. Reduce heat and leave to simmer. Separate the eggs. Beat the egg whites until stiff. Drop spoonfuls into the heated milk. When each spoonful of egg white has cooked on one side, turn over to cook on the other side. Place cooked egg whites on top of layered biscuits. Beat the separated egg yolks plus extra egg yolks and add sugar, vanilla, cornflour and two tablespoons of milk. Beat together then add to the leftover milk in which the egg whites were cooked. Heat and cook until mixture thickens into a custard. Pour custard over egg whites and biscuits. Sprinkle with grated chocolate (or grated lemon rind if preferred). Serves 6–8.

Duties were divided in a traditional way, by sex. The men did the roasting and drinking and the women were on baking and table setting. Long tables were set up in the winery and covered with white cloths, white plates and red serviettes. Water glasses were provided for the wine as in the countryside in France, and two-gallon bottles of white and red wine labelled 'White Wine' and 'Red Wine' were placed at intervals. Huge baskets of homemade country bread appeared as more and more people began to arrive to help and share in the party. Two teatree fires had been lit for the two lambs, and the beasts were being prepared on a large table. Kruno stabbed deep cuts into the carcasses into which he stuffed salt, garlic and

BOSNIAN ČEVAĆCIĆI

500 g FINELY MINCED TOPSIDE BEEF
500 g MINCED PORK
2 CLOVES GARLIC, CRUSHED
1 tsp SALT
1 tsp PEPPER
½ tsp BAKING SODA
2 ONIONS

Mix both meats together in a bowl. Add garlic, salt, pepper, baking soda and mix well. Leave to stand for about two hours. Form small sausages about 5 cm long and 2 cm diameter, by rolling the meat mixture between the palms of your hands. The Čevaćciči can be cooked under a grill or on a barbecue or in a heavy frypan lightly oiled. Cook until brown all over. Serve on a platter with roughly chopped raw onions. Serves 6.

For a slightly hotter variation from Serbia — Pljeskavice — use the standard Čevaćciči mixture but add one to four chopped pickled chilli peppers, three extra cloves of crushed garlic and a pinch of chilli powder. Stand for two hours, then form into round flat patties and cook as before.

sprigs of rosemary, then the whole thing was rubbed with salt. They yelled at each other about which way it should be done, while George and I stood by and laughed. Everybody gave orders and nobody obeyed them. The front hocks were chopped off and used to twist the abdominal cavity closed, then the tongue of the animal was cut out and a teatree stick passed up through the body, past the slit throat and out the mouth.

I went upstairs to Jordanka's kitchen to see what was going on in the baking department. The kitchen was full of warm-hearted women in white lacy aprons, drinking tea and preparing food. The crew were squashed in there for our cooking demonstration and being treated to freshly deep-fried Krostule — pastry strips cut into triangles that are pulled through a centre slit, then fried and drenched in icing sugar. All the women call you sweetheart and darling and touch you when they speak, their eyes sparking with *joi de vivre*.

'You got very unusual skin, sweetheart,' said Jessie.

'Mmm, it's called an Irish polka,' I replied.

'We all learned to cook very young,' said Dunya, 'because everybody in the family worked. We all had to help in and out of the house before we could go out and play. I am trying to do less but here I am on the Dalmatian Society committee.'

'Peta, we saw you on the show last night,' said Celina. 'We don't care that the fish don't work. We like you because you a natural girl.'

I had to get the pronunciation right for the interview with Vojna Pavlovich.

'It's not possible that you haven't got a bit of Dally in you somewhere, Peta,' they shouted, 'because you know how to say our names.' I could hear singing and accordion-playing wafting up from downstairs and was itching to get down there. Meantime, for the camera, the adorable Vojna made her famous *Rizhot od Lignja* or squid risotto. She almost died of nervousness but managed to get a few sentences out. She uses the squid ink in her risotto, which is a typical dish from her area and obviously of Italian origin. It is absolutely delicious.

PETA AND VOJNA HAVING THE BEST TIME PREPARING *RIZHOT OD LIGNJA*.

VOJNA'S *RIZHOT OD LIGNJA*

4 FEMALE SQUID WITH THE INK SACKS

1 cup SHORT GRAIN OR ITALIAN RISOTTO RICE

OLIVE OIL

2 ONIONS, CHOPPED

3 CLOVES OF GARLIC, CHOPPED

1/2 cup OF PARSLEY, FINELY CHOPPED

1 medium can TOMATO SOUP

1 tbsp PAPRIKA

2 tsp VEGETA (YUGOSLAV VEGETABLE STOCK) AVAILABLE FROM SEAMART

SALT AND FRESHLY GROUND PEPPER

Slice and clean squid and boil for one minute in salted water. Remove squid and retain cooking liquid. Cook the rice in the squid water. When cooked it should be of a sticky consistency like in a risotto. Heat some olive oil and sauté the onions and garlic till golden then add the squid, parsley, tomato soup, paprika, vegeta, and squid ink. Mix the rice and squid mixture together and season to taste.

As soon as we had finished I ran downstairs to the music. I had hardly set foot in the room when food was pressed on me. How could I refuse? I gave it to others because I couldn't bear to say no. People pressed wine on me. How could I refuse? OK, so I drank it but only out of politeness. More people had arrived and half of them belonged to the Dalmatian choir. There were three accordionists playing with people standing around them singing emotional, passionate songs in three- and four-part harmony. The music was very potent, like a deep, deep flowing river impregnated in people's veins. They sang with their arms around one another, sometimes dancing, sometimes almost weeping. I was so moved by these beautiful songs I was almost in tears myself. Franka Tihana (the quiet one), who had the most powerful voice I have ever heard, sang 'Zora'. There was a wonderful song about a baby who didn't look anything like its father but awfully like the neighbour, and a gut-wrenching one about a fisherman at which half the room practically lay down on the floor with the pathos of it. The old ladies were in the front row in full throttle.

tHE FISHERMAN'S SONG

The fisherman mends his net
Which he needs for himself.
Who will mend it tomorrow?
He doesn't really care.

Sing this song old fisherman
Because this is a song of the sea.

Divine sea, blue sea,
You are my dear one.
You are my heart's desire,
You are my richness.

Divine pear of my homeland,
Your beauty overwhelms me.

rIBAR PLETE

Ribar plete mrižu svoju
Koja njemu triba
A ko `ce je sutra plesti
Bas ga nije briga

Zapivaj pismuribare stari
Jer to je pisma o moru

More divno more plavo
Ti si meni drago
Ti si čežnja srca moga
Ti si moje blago

Biseru divini rodnog mi kraj
Lipota tvoja me opaja.

On a table was laid out an assortment of delicacies such as home-made *Strudel*, almond *Torte*, *Kolace* (almond crescents), *Palachinke* (pancakes), cheese *Pitas*, *Salane Sardele* (sardines marinated in olive oil and onions), *Prsut* (prosciutto) and *Rozata* (cream caramel). The strong, country wine was being passed around in *bukaras*, the communal wooden mug. I wandered over to the barbecue department, which by this stage was a lot looser than earlier on. Shirts were off, wine was seriously on, as was story telling, and the beasts were well on their way. The fire had settled down to embers and had been spread on to corrugated iron sheets. The lambs had been placed on old boxes at each end to roast gently and were constantly basted using a rag tied to a teatree pole. The rag was dipped in a mixture of lemon juice, wine, salt and rosemary by the cooks, some of whom sat at each end turning the spit and telling stories.

Traditionally, the head of the sheep is left on and is considered a great delicacy. At weddings in the old country, it was placed on a platter and passed around the table. The person who put the most money on the tray was lucky enough to get the head. Finally, the moment arrived when our lamb was cooked, cut up and placed on the tables on huge dishes along with potatoes that had been cooked in pans in the cinders.

'I suppose you're used to fancier food than this,' said Berta, in between singing her heart out and eating. The hard core crooners just couldn't bear to stop singing and carried on throughout the meal.

'Yes, but nothing can replace the taste of food made with love, songs sung with passion and hospitality given with an open heart,' I replied, stuffing myself with the tender, succulent lamb. 'I would eat plastic bags if I liked the host.'

Conversations got louder and more political as the wine flowed. People fell off their chairs on top of each other singing nationalistic Tito songs. Men harangued me with their opinions of the situation in what was Yugoslavia, their terrible, terrible pain and impotence blackening their eyes. The women told them to shut up, and most of them seemed to feel that it was more important for the Dalmatian community in New Zealand to be united, no matter what their ethnic origin. George was smiling and trying to explain what people were saying to me. The bond with the homeland was every bit as powerful as Kruno's country wine, and the more that wine slipped down, the closer home became.

At the end of the feast, George stood up and yelled his head off for a while till he got everyone to be quiet, then started in on the thank yous. These were followed by thank you songs both to our hosts Jordanka and Kruno and to the *Town & Country* team, which prompted Chris to leap up and announce that I would thank them with a song of my own. I sang 'Hymne a l'Amour', a Piaf love song in which she places herself at her lover's feet with all sorts of preposterous declarations.

*f*or you I would unhook the moon.
For you I would steal a fortune.
For you I would betray my country.
For you I would dye my hair blonde.

OK, I can see betraying your country for a man, but to dye your hair? Please. My song was thanked with a deluge of kisses, smiles and arms being wrapped around me. I was forthwith issued an invitation to come back and sing with the Dalmatian choir, which I accepted with pleasure.

At about six-thirty I went outside to find the crew holding up the front of the house, giggling.

'Another production meeting?' I enquired.

They collapsed and said, 'Well yes actually, it's about you. We can't see you getting away from this lot inside three days, so we're looking for a taxi chit for you.'

'Don't be silly,' I said gaily. 'I'm absolutely ready to leave now. I've heard thirty-seven different versions of Yugoslav history and I don't really think I can take on board another one. As the honourable saying goes — he who hesitates is last!'

the first thing they tried to make me do on the Puhoi (Bohemian word meaning slow water) shoot was jump in a canoe and paddle down the river. Nope said I. Fine said they. Cody and Kathryn Mankelow and their extremely cute baby leapt without further ado into one of their bullet-proof, untippable canoes and sailed off into the delicate veil of rain. It's hard to imagine the unspeakable hardship of the original settlers on this river, when one sees how easy Cody and Kathryn make it for the punters in their river-rafting business called The Puhoi River Canoe Hire. They pick up their canoeists from Wenderholm at the end of the trip or deliver them there for the voyage up the river with the incoming tide. The canoes are loaded back on to the trailer and the intrepid sailors are delivered back to their cars. One paddles through the mangroves and tamed bush admiring the herons, pukeko and kingfishers and doesn't even feel the past — the past that saw people on the verge of starvation, so hard was the bush and their lives.

The picturesque, European-style village of Puhoi is only thirty miles (48 kilometres) north of Auckland, but in the old days it may as well have been three hundred, so complete was the isolation, both geographic and linguistic. In 1863 about eighty Bohemians arrived in New Zealand. They had come halfway around the world from several villages southwest of Prague in the kingdom of Bohemia, which is now part of Czechoslovakia. In 1863 Bohemia was a province in the northern part of the Austrian Empire. They spoke a dialect called *Eghalander* and also German, were staunch Catholics and farmers looking for land and a better life. They had been told that New Zealand was a land where there was no hunger, no poverty and no winter. They were in for a terrible shock and nothing could hide their horror but they couldn't go back as they had used all their money to get here. One woman said, 'If I could have walked on water I would have turned around and walked home.' They were faced with impenetrable bush, non-existent housing and the disadvantage of not speaking English. However, they prevailed and succeeded in taming the land and creating a community by helping each other and sticking to their strong religious faith.

As usual, the women worked the hardest, rising at 3 am to do the housework, cook the breakfast and organise the children. They then worked beside their men all morning doing manual labour, returned home at midday to cook lunch, went back to work in the afternoon, then back home to cook dinner. Oh and in between, in their spare time, they endured numerous pregnancies and childbirths. When one of Mrs Russek's children broke a leg, she carried the child on her back to Auckland along hilly tracks through the forest. One of the rare times they were able to rise above their hard lives was when they danced, and it is this tradition plus some Bohemian dishes that have survived to this day.

When they danced, they DANCED and sometimes it went on for a week. To the music of fiddles, *dudelsacks* (a primitive sort of horn pipe) and button accordions, they got dressed up and flung themselves into the polka, the *schottische* and the *dumadum*. We filmed the Puhoi Bohemian Dancers stepping out a lovely *Eghalander* polka on the street outside the old church. In this fast dance there is a formation where two men are in the middle with two women on the outside. They link arms turning round and round, the women flying with their feet about a foot off the ground showing off their snowy white, hand-made socks. The women wore white, lacy blouses with full, puffed sleeves covered by intricately embroidered and beaded

PUHOI VALLEY CHEESES.

bodices. Full skirts with lacy petticoats, colourful scarves and little, black, buckled shoes completed the look. Not an inch of skin was in sight save for a bit of arm.

The tiny, wooden church of Saints Peter and Paul, built in 1881, bears the names of the founders like Schischka and Schollum, and it was in this church my family heard Sunday Mass in the summer when we were children. Puhoi these days is probably most famous for its lovely old pub, frequented by locals, visitors and bikers. Photographs of early Puhoi, bullock horns and old farming and logging equipment cover the walls.

After pies and hamburgers for lunch, we set off to the famous Puhoi Valley Cheese Company. We had to go through three different doors just to get inside, each chamber landmined with special white clothes, hand-scrubbing troughs, sheep dips (antiseptic gumboot baths), airlocks and air purification systems. It was like visiting a prison or the infectious disease unit of a nuclear plant.

BRIE, ANYONE?

I looked at Laurence. 'I feel like saying "yes, I've come to see my husband. He's the one who killed ten grandmothers with a chainsaw,"' I confided as I slipped my shoes off and left my bags outside. 'You know what I mean? It's a bit like Paremoremo.'

'Actually, Peta, no, I wouldn't know what being in Paremoremo is like,' he replied. 'How is it you have such privileged information?'

'For your edification, I used to visit prisoners in Paremoremo because I had a thing called a social conscience. My boyfriend was a criminal lawyer with a feel for the underdog.'

'I think it's more like a hospital really.'

'The Greeks make cheese with flies crawling all over it and it basically walks to the table on its own. What's the big deal with all this hygiene? I'm very suspicious of people obsessed with cleanliness.'

'It's next to godliness.'

'Exactly.'

Cleansed to within an inch of our lives and clad in shower caps, white coats and white gumboots, we finally approached the inner sanctum.

'This outfit reminds me of my days at Auckland Hospital,' I said to Richard the soundman.

'God. I thought you were joking when you said you were a brain surgeon.'

I soon got told in no uncertain terms by the charming manager

Corrie den Haring that some people have standards and *some* people don't wish to poison the public and anyway it's the law of the land. Now, this business of mandatory pasteurisation of milk for cheese making is a bone of contention with me. I cannot tell a lie. The cheese can't grow and develop intense flavours and interesting vintages if there are no bugs in it, as the French have known for centuries, so in New Zealand we are obliged to add artificial starters. The pro-pasteuriser's camp say it ensures consistency of the product and zero deaths from Listeria. The anti-pasteuriser's camp (usually boutique producers) say large companies are more concerned to protect their export industry than the consumer.

Cheese expert Juliet Harbutt finds it 'infuriating beyond belief' that all New Zealand cheeses have to be made from pasteurised milk, arguing that unpasteurised does not mean dirty. Like me, Harbutt is passionately in love with cheese and doesn't see why we can't make hand-made cheeses wrapped in leaves and stored in caves. She believes small producers should not be subject to the same unbending and expensive inspections as the big players.

But enough ranting and back to Puhoi Cheeses. Do they stand up, so to speak? I was kindly given a selection, prompting my friends and me to form a tasting panel the next Sunday afternoon with the help of some health-enhancing red wine. The soft, white rind cheeses like Camembert and Brie were moist but not runny enough — they needed more time to sit around, but the goat's cheese feta, one of their original products, was deliciously salty and creamy. The ricotta was fresh and sweet and I loved the Quarg (from the German *quark*). Quarg (hence the word quagmire) is a fresh, soft cheese related to yoghurt, cream cheese and cottage cheese with the consistency of a thick, gloopy paste. It is low in calories, high in protein and utterly delicious. You can make sweets with it, put it in pies, eat it on its own with honey and thicken sauces with it.

Puhoi Cheese have quite a big factory really, with all sorts of flash new equipment. Owner Lloyd Darroch started production in 1983, selling one ton of goat cheese in the first year. After a few lean years and just about to give up, he heard about a machine that extracted whey from milk. This ultra-filtration system produces a much thicker, creamier milk that speeds up the cheese-making process, increases the yield and often results in a better end product. He bought the equipment, got in some experts and is now New Zealand's top producer of specialty cheeses, using both cow's and goat's milk. The cheeses are concocted from milk still warm from the udder, hand-made and individually wrapped by pretty maids all in a row.

Being so clean, we decided to cook something, so we drove off to find Jenny Schollum who was going to make us her *Kochen* or Bohemian Cheesecake. Some other traditional dishes are still made, for instance *Hunky-Punky* (deep-fried scones), *Sauerkraut* and Fat Roast. By this time, we were all starting to get tired, slightly tetchy and dodgy in the concentration department. It was the fifth straight day of filming, the weather was very hot and very humid and I didn't need hangers-on standing around staring at me. I started committing criminal offences, like wandering across a shoot in a daze and not being able to memorise my pieces to camera, an act I felt I had been finally getting a handle on. Jenny, a gentle, nervous creature, made the *Kochen*, and thankfully we sat down and ate it with tea before we all turned into werewolves.

JENNY SCHOLLUM'S *KOCHEN*

250 g SWEET, SHORT PASTRY OR SCONE DOUGH

500 g QUARG

1 tbsp SUGAR

2 EGGS, BEATEN

1 tbsp SULTANAS

1 tbsp FLOUR

1 tsp MELTED BUTTER

PLUM JAM

FRESH CREAM TO SERVE

Roll out the pastry or scone dough into a round about the size of a small pizza and 1 cm thick. Place on a greased oven tray. Mix together the quarg, sugar, eggs, sultanas, flour and butter and spread over the base. Dot several teaspoons of plum jam over the top and bake at 190°C for about thirty minutes. Whilst the cheesecake is still warm, pour a little cream over the top and serve.

AFTERNOON TEA WITH JENNY
SCHOLLUM.

Raising our blood sugar made us nice again, which was the very
moment a reporter turned up from the local paper to take photos.

'Do you need us to be in the photo?' enquired Laurence casually.

'Well, no, if you wouldn't mind terribly,' the lovely lady replied
politely, 'after all, Peta is the star. She's the one they'll all be wanting
to see.'

Deathly silence.

I turned my head to the crew in barely controlled triumph and
nodded it with flaring nostrils.

'Could you repeat that, Margaret?' I gloated, which she did to
their sneering, guffawing countenances.

'Of course,' I confided to her, 'you know I would be nothing
without them.'

'Bloody right you wouldn't. Some might say you're nothing *with*
us,' he who shall remain unnamed suggested. HE KNOWS WHO HE IS.
(I got that line from Sister Rose at Holy Cross Convent. She would
say 'there's a certain element in this school AND THEY KNOW WHO THEY
ARE' whereupon my eyes would automatically cross.)

LAKE GRASSMERE (SALT LAKE).

blenheim

p *iu se spenne, peggio se magna —* the more you spend, the less well you eat

On the plane down to Blenheim, Laurence said to me, 'If you're not on the edge, you're taking up too much room.'

'That is very deep,' I replied, watching the (in-the-unlikely-event) crash drill intently.

'Also, please buy your own bottle of gin from now on.'

'That is very superficial and I don't consider it dignifies your person.'

'Why are you listening to the flight attendant?'

'This could be the day of a "pilot error".'

'It's a one-in-a-million chance. Have a gin.'

'How kind.'

i have only good memories of Blenheim. The first time I went there was as a guest of the *Listener* Women's Book Festival and then again on a double bill with Sam Hunt at Hunter's Vintner's restaurant during the Marlborough Food and Wine Festival. I was singing Piaf songs and Sam was saying his poetry, which to the uninitiated might sound like an unlikely combination on the same day in the same space. However, thanks to the generosity of Blenheim diners and the unmitigated unpretentiousness of Sam, they were great nights.

Believe it or not, I had never seen Sam perform live before in spite of the fact that we had been brought up in the same era and the same town. Upon interrogation, it turned out he had gone to the same school as my brothers — St Peters. He walked out and headed south, never to look back. I found him to be a well-spoken, loving, intelligent and polite man. He is incredibly widely read and his own and other people's poetry pepper his conversation as naturally as olive oil goes with pasta. He stood up whenever a woman addressed him at his table and made every person he talked to feel they had enriched his life. Which is not to say he suffers fools gladly because he doesn't.

Sam fretted about the bad microphone and was very clear about how long he would talk and when he would talk. I am so used to impossible performing situations that a microphone seemed like a pebble under a mattress. His performance was riveting, real, old-style poetry recitation and all of it was from memory. He was dressed in white 'Foxton straights', white shirt open halfway down his chest, long shell necklace, bracelet and Doc Marten boots, and his hairdo was anarchy in motion. When people requested their favourites, he beat time by stamping or slapping his thighs and delivered his lines in that famous nicotine-gravel voice. Some of the poems made you laugh, some of them made you cry and lots of them made you think. He recited some James K. Baxter numbers and told the story of how Baxter taught him to make 'steam' if he was stuck in a motel room in the middle of nowhere with nothing left to drink. First you go out and buy some meths and a packet of sliced bread from the nearest possible location. Then you toast a few slices of bread till they're black — it works better if you remove the plastic packaging. Pour meths through burnt toast and add a little orange juice. NB — please don't consider this the first recipe of the chapter. It's just a bit of cultural history. And meths can make you go blind.

Sam, of course, has no need of this recipe as he stopped drinking years ago, and being sober hasn't adversely affected his poetry or his ability to perform. His partner Amanda, a handsome, warm, calm woman, was with him, nodding her head in time to the beat of his words. Friends of mine who were also old acquaintances of Sam's had come down from Auckland for the wine festival, provoked by the additional titillation of having both Sam and me on the same stage. They stayed in a house that they told me was remarkable for its appalling decor and liver-coloured toilets. Sam and Amanda stayed in a caravan in the vineyard and I stayed at Jane Hunter's place.

Jane Hunter is an interesting woman because she seems so young to be heading the successful empire of Hunter's Wines. Well known for her generosity and public spirit, she opened her lovely home to me, wrote constant notes about the whereabouts of food (eat what you want, do what you want), loaned me a car for the duration of my stay and was unfailingly charming. She's the sort of woman who has expensive body lotions in the guest bathroom and Lapsang Souchong tea in the kitchen. As well as running the winery, she has the restaurant, travels constantly to speak, promote New Zealand and Hunter's wines, judge awards and do tastings and has this year set up an artist's lodge on her property for an artist in residence to work. I braved the wine festival on the Saturday, which resembled a huge English country fair, wherein I got more wine chucked over me than at an adolescent Friday night. There were so many people that we had to queue for ages to get a morsel to eat and queue for ages to use a toilet. For me these huge crowd scenes are just not worth it. The truly wonderful thing about Marlborough vineyards, though, is that the vines are planted just wide enough apart to park a car and they stretch as far as the eye can see.

Here I was back again in sunny Blenheim on the food trail for Taste New Zealand. Chris was already holed up in the hotel inventing a script, so Laurence and I went off to borrow plates from Levenes and visit our future victims. Our first stop was the award-winning Rocco's, an Italian restaurant on Dodson Road. I had always tried to eat here on my visits to Blenheim but could never get in. We were greeted by a big man with a big smile and an accent straight out of an Anna Magnani film — the adorable Piero Rocco. I can't talk about Piero and Barbara Rocco without excessive affection and admiration so you'll just have to put up with it. When you go there, and you will, once you have read this chapter, you will see that everything about them is generous, not least of all their hearts.

The restaurant doesn't look like anything special on the outside, but walk in and you're in a traditional *trattoria* in Venice. Cured *prosciutto* hams hang from the ceiling along with garlic and dried flowers tied with red ribbons. At one end of the room is a large tank full of Piero's friends — crayfish that are all named and never to be eaten. An open fire with a spit for roasting meat has pride of place at the other end of the large restaurant, which is decorated in the old-fashioned way with red tablecloths, embossed velvet chairs, Chianti bottles and red candles. There is a piano and a terrace with even more tables.

In the garden grows a huge olive tree laden with fruit that the Rocco's planted thirteen years ago. The kitchen is very simple with a sign on the door leading from it to the restaurant that says 'hit this door at 5000 smiles an hour'. The cool room is out the back, along with the store room overflowing with olive oil, anchovies, sun-dried tomatoes, capers, flour, wine, etc. We dispensed with going over what we would be filming the next day and what food would be required. I hadn't eaten since my freezing sandwich on the plane, it was now four o'clock and I was shifting from foot to foot. As we were leaving I said,

'Piero, there's just one more thing — I'm starving to death. Would I be able to have a piece of bread with a few slices of your *prosciutto*?'

'You hungry?' Piero exclaimed. 'Is-a no problem. We make you something. Is-a my pleasure.'

He leaned over the kitchen server and spoke to one of the chefs. I saw her getting out smoked salmon, melon and grapes from the fridge.

'No, no Piero, I don't want a big deal — just a snack. A ham sandwich is all I want,' I insisted.

'Is-a no trouble, Peta, is just a little plate,' he laughed, 'and of course you'll need some wine.'

Laurence and I looked at each other.

'Well . . . maybe just one glass.'

Have you ever been looking forward to something so much, your salivary glands actually hurt? Needless to say, a bottle of his house Gewürztraminer 1995 labelled 'Crayfish Juice' arrived along with a platter of *Tapenade*, fresh tomato chopped up with herbs and onion, thin slices of *prosciutto*, smoked salmon, melon, grapes and garlic bread. Piero sat down with us and we heard a little of his story.

He was a master mariner who served sixteen years as a captain and senior pilot with the Venice Harbour Authority. He met and fell in love with Barbara, a New Zealander, when she was there on holiday. They got married, had a baby and eventually came to New Zealand to live. In 1995 Rocco's won best South Island restaurant along with Oliver's in Clyde. Piero is very involved with the Lions and Barbara is president of IHC. They have received many awards for their dedication to humanitarian services. Every hand movement, every eye flicker, every word from this man's mouth showed how much he loves life. He lives and breathes Marlborough and can't believe his luck to be living in such a beautiful, wonderful place. He has a vineyard, goes fishing on Sundays and is crazy about all the primary products Marlborough provides for his kitchen.

The *prosciutto* or cured ham entirely lived up to my expectations. I closed my eyes and I was in the Italian restaurant I cooked in in Paris, slicing Parma ham and wrapping it around giant prawns. There is nothing to beat a thick slice of country bread, covered in butter and piled up with paper thin slices of cured ham. Piero's

Crayfish Juice made from his own grapes was concocted by his friends at Johanneshoff Wines, whom we decided to pay a visit in the hope that we would be back next year with *Town & Country*.

There was no signage for Johanneshoff, so we drove right past a few times before finally asking for instructions. An unprepossessing house came into view with its small vineyard of dark-red grapes hidden shyly behind white veils. Edel (German) and Warwick (Marlboroughite) are a couple in love with each other and winemaking. In their German-style tasting room, they gave us a taste of what turned out to be Piero's Crayfish Juice with a different label, then a peek at their famous cave. They told us they like to do things the traditional, long-hand way, but nothing could have prepared us for the sight that awaited behind the Belle Epoque iron gate.

Count Dracula's chamber unfolded before our eyes — a damp, rocky tunnel lit by candles in ornate antique holders attached to the walls, which had been blasted and dug out by miners. Along one side were trestle-shaped holders with slanted holes in them, at a suitable angle to lodge wine bottles. These they had bought from Veuve Cliquot. We tasted some beautiful Cognac from the barrel then moved on down to the end of the tunnel where there was an alcove filled with bottles of wine symmetrically stacked four feet (1.2 metres) high with the help of thin slats of wood. Next a key was produced and we were ushered with all due ceremony into the inner chamber. This is the tunnel where the serious action happens and where their private collection lives and breathes. Here the penicillin had gone completely overboard and was oozing and fulminating its white growth all over the wine bottles. It was crawling down the walls looking everywhere, in my opinion, for a piece of cheese. It would be a great place to grow button mushrooms also and, in fact, I did see

WARWICK AND EDEL'S PERSONAL WINE COLLECTION.

fleshy, white mushrooms growing on the wall that resembled *pleurottes*.

At the end of this tunnel was a glistening upended barrel with tasting glasses on it and candles in a three-pronged, silver candle-holder. It was all so romantic and idealistic, and Edel and Warwick were entrancing in the way they spoke of not wanting to lose the heart and soul of Marlborough winemaking. Like Piero, they have a genuine love of the area, the earth, the lifestyle and the wine, unlike others who appear to be in the business for the bucks and the kudos. Warwick is an intense, nice looking man dressed in blue overalls, and Edel has a great nose and amazing, slanted, green eyes. She is softly spoken and highly educated in terms of winemaking, being the fifth generation in her family to follow this vocation. Warwick opened one of his Méthode Champenoise and, well, we were locked in the cave, so we had to drink it. This loosened conversation up considerably.

'Do you have any children?' Laurence asked.

'No. Not yet,' replied Warwick, hastening to add, 'not that I'm shooting blanks or anything like that.'

'I am,' said Laurence, 'and I love it.'

'Yes well, thank you very much from the family planning clinic,' I said, 'moving right along.'

We emerged into the sunlight feeling much the better for wear, with great hopes to meet again.

Our cameraman and sound man, both called Chris, for heaven's sake, arrived from Wellington the next morning. From then on the Chrises were known as chief-Chris, sound-Chris and camera-Chris, all three of them being united by their niceness. I got togged up in a little white silk netting dress with black slip and we started the day off at Ponder Estate in search of the humble olive, the same humble olive that is rapidly becoming a fashionable and successful commercial venture in New Zealand. I predict that olive growing and olive-oil pressing will move as fast as winemaking has. The Greeks, who attributed a divine origin to olives, venerated them so much that for a long time the only people who were employed in the cultivation of this tree were virgin women and pure men. An oath of chastity was required by those who were charged with harvesting the crop. I didn't question Mike Ponder on the suitability of his harvesters. Mike and Diane, who also have a vineyard producing Sauvignon Blanc and Chardonnay, were amongst the first in New Zealand to see the potential of an olive-oil industry in Marlborough. They first planted in 1988 with olive trees from Israel, and the first commercial pressing was in 1994. The 1995 crop was tested at a remarkable 0.20 per cent oleic acid (acidity) and is extra virgin, which means there is only one cold pressing — what you get is the best.

We wandered around the olive groves trying to catch each other's voices — he is six foot six (that's almost 2 metres, though I had been told eight foot or about 2.44 metres) and I am five foot four (about 1.63 metres).

'My favourite recipe is filling a jug with olive oil and dipping bread into it,' confided Mike.

'Really?' I replied. 'Mine is filling a jug with olive oil, pouring it all over my favourite person and licking it all off.'

He looked at me.

'Can I put that in my book?'

'Be my guest. But of course,' I admitted, 'you would have to really like olive oil.'

'You'd have to really like the person,' Chris laughed.

'You could end up hating both olive oil and the person,' Mike suggested. He gets up to a hundred letters a week from people asking his advice on how to grow olives, so he's writing a book on it.

Olives are a mysterious fruit and I'd love to know who figured out how to make them edible. Straight off the tree, they are vile, but in their various transformations they are heavenly. The difference between green and black is simply the ripeness. Olives have been cultivated for over 6000 years and there are hundreds of varieties. They were originally grown in the Mediterranean and North Africa, and in Italy there are still groves that are 2000 years old. The free-draining soil of Marlborough is great for olives as are the long, hot summers. Mike grows fifteen varieties now — some are used for pickling and some for oil — and they're hand harvested in July. Ponder olives are pressed in Blenheim as they don't have their own press. Up at the Shed Gallery where you can taste oil, olives, *tapenade*, wine and peruse Mike's paintings, I sat and drank the oil by the spoonful. It is a soft green colour with a nutty, herbacious flavour and delightfully peppery after taste. Their oil is unfiltered to retain its flavour, nutrition and character. Try it drizzled over *bocconcini* (Mozzarella cheese) or your favourite person.

I assume lunch was a pie because I don't remember eating it. Our next stop involved mountains of garlic and the beautiful Thelma Sowman of Wairau Products at Kaituna. They grow garlic and shallots and garlic and shallots and garlic and shallots. Garlic loves Marlborough. It loves the cold winters and dry, hot summers. It's planted in mid-winter, the planting sometimes going on all night, and harvested in mid-summer. Marlborough grows most of New Zealand's garlic and exports 60 per cent of it to Australia, Fiji, Tahiti and New Caledonia. Like olives, garlic has been around for a long time, dating back to 2000BC. They say that slaves working on the great pyramids downed tools when their garlic supply was stopped. They believed it gave them strength and protected them from illness. I find that my slaves won't do a thing without it. Its medicinal properties are well known — it lowers cholesterol, prevents bowel cancer, is an antibiotic, thins the blood, cures colds and sore throats and gets rid of anybody standing within a mile of you.

The taste of garlic is detectable on the skin up to seventy-two hours after ingestion, but Thelma has that sorted out. She says eat parsley or suck on a lemon — that absorbs the smell. Not so the delectable, refined shallot. It's only recently that we have been able to get a decent shallot in New Zealand but they are used a lot in Europe. With their reddish-brown skins, small size and delicate, aromatic flavour, these gourmet onions can be used wherever you might use an onion. They're great for sauces because they melt easily, perfect for vinaigrettes and sweet in salads. Thelma showed us how she roasts whole heads of garlic. Don't be afraid to try this. Roasted garlic loses its tang and becomes sweet and mellow. It's very good with roasted lamb and free-range chicken.

ROASTED GARLIC BULBS

GARLIC BULBS
OLIVE OIL
CHOPPED BASIL, THYME AND OREGANO
SALT AND FRESHLY GROUND PEPPER

Slice the top quarter off the bulbs to expose the cloves. Puncture the sides and top with a fork. Drizzle lots of olive oil over them and sprinkle with the herbs and salt and pepper. Put in a small oven-proof dish and bake at 180°C for an hour. Baste occasionally. To serve, squeeze the soft cloves out of the skins and *voila*! You can actually buy ceramic containers expressly for this purpose from kitchenware shops.

What hangs around in secluded places, doesn't need feeding or fertiliser and earns more than fifty million dollars a year in overseas exchange for Marlborough and New Zealand? No, not rugby players, silly — greenshell mussels! Garlic goes really well with mussels but mussels are not born in supermarkets as most people think. Oh no. Would it were so simple! Mussels have to be prised from mucky pieces of rope to which they cling desperately. Two or three days each week, Grant Godsiff helms the *Wilderness Express* trip out on the mussel run. The principal reason for the journey is a water-testing programme, but for the price of a ticket anyone can join them, which is what we decided to do. Marlborough calls itself a gourmet paradise, and their largest earner is mussel farming and processing to the tune of 8000 tonnes per year, based at Havelock. The Sounds have always been popular, but the deep, clear waters produce more than happy tourists. The purity of the water has enabled salmon to be farmed without the use of antibiotics or bacteriocides.

We sped out to the crystal waters with our blue-eyed, white-haired, pipe-smoking, salty dog at the helm. As you approach the Sounds, you see hundreds of mussel buoys lined up like rows of

schoolboys in black uniforms. Six hundred farms are dotted about the Sounds, and I haven't a clue how they tell one farm from another. What happens is baby mussels called spats are collected from coastal waters around New Zealand and grown on ropes till they are 30 mm long, then they're stripped off and seeded on to vertical ropes attached to the buoyed surface ropes, where they grow to maturity. They draw all the necessities of life from the Sounds' tidal flow, and the whole process from spathood to adulthood takes eighteen months. The laden, seaweed-dripping ropes are winched up by twin-engined, purpose-built boats, and the mussels are removed and transported to the factory in one tonne bags.

The next really weird place we found ourselves in was somewhere you would never go if you enjoyed communicating with other human beings — a mussel-processing factory. You have this vision of a quiet, ordered little job, right? How much noise can a mussel make, right? The answer is mussels make such a racket you actually have to wear headphones. It's not that they are begging for their lives and screaming, or anything macabre like that. It's that the shells, when being chucked around by the tonne, make an incredible racket. Rows and rows of blue-and-white attired workers sorted and opened the mussels, repeating the same movement over and over again. You can't even gossip and create lies about your neighbour to make it tolerable. I watched in fascination as workers filled their boxes, some faster than others. In this factory (Sanford's) mussels were processed into either half shell, mussel meat, marinated, frozen whole or packed live to be sold all over the world.

there is a God after all, and (s)he found a table for us at Rocco's that night for dinner. We perused a very comprehensive wine list and decided to start off with Piero's Crayfish Juice for old times' sake. The entrée had been decided by Piero, so all we had to do was wait in happy anticipation. This meal rated up there with the feast at Daniel's Orient in Dunedin for hospitality. A huge selection of entrées arrived, borne by the green-grey-eyed Barbara. After grilled prawns, scallops, salmon, salami, salad and garlic bread, we moved on to *Frascati Superiore*. Every so often, Piero ran out to ask if everything was all right, then ran smiling back into the kitchen again. I ordered lamb rack for my main, which came simply roasted with home-made pasta. Piero doesn't like to serve a sauce with the lamb because the quality is too good to disguise. With it I drank a beautiful 1993 Rosso Conero from Umbria. Laurence and Chris ordered fish, which came with a saying: 'Fish must always swim three times. The first time in the sea. The second time in olive oil. The third time in your stomach in the wine you drink with it.'

Piero and Barbara joined us after dinner, bringing with them a gift of a 1988 Cloudy Bay Cabernet Merlot.

'But there're no more of these left!' we all gasped.

'At a-Rocco's there are,' beamed Piero.

It was such a clever wine — very round, lots of nose and long lasting. Veuve Cliquot now own 71 per cent of Cloudy Bay and the deal is they cannot interfere with the winemaker, Kevin Judd.

'You know, I was in a-Venice at a wine tasting and the French were very agitated about the Cloudy Bay. I went over to the table and stole a glass and admitted I lived down a-the road from this winery. Everyone looked at me in a-wonder.'

Piero's food is simple, old-style Italian cooking, completely free from pretension and inundated with freshness. Barbara, a small grey-haired woman with very sparkly eyes, appeared to be completely in love with her husband.

'He's the creative one,' she said, 'I'm the sensible one.'

'I have made you a special dessert,' announced Piero.

'Oh no, we can't eat any more. We are going to die,' I groaned.

'Thank you, we'd love dessert,' said Chris.

Home-made *Tiramisu* arrived surrounded by home-made *Zabaglione Gelato*, which was to die for and I *did* manage just a spoon or two. After that we really were finished but, no, the evening was not yet over.

'Just a little something to end off with,' said Piero. 'It's not sweet but comforting.'

Home-made *biscotti* were dipped into little glasses of port and handed to us as we talked about Venice and history and the meaning of life. I think you should always save the light subjects for last, that way you can't remember the nonsense you said the next day. Barbara is always trying to get Piero to slow down, but somehow it hasn't worked yet.

'Life's too short to have willpower,' she laughed. When he watched her speaking, Piero's head sort of inclined and he looked like someone just gave him a puppy.

■

In Roman times soldiers were paid in salt, hence the word salary and the saying 'a man is worth his salt'. Salt comes from four main sources. The first is sea-salt, the processing of which we filmed at Lake Grassmere. The second is rock-salt, which is mined like coal. The underground mines are where you went to work in Russia if you had written anti-party literature. The third is brine-well-salt, which is produced by sinking a well like an oil-well into the rock-salt deposit. Fresh water is forced down to dissolve the salt and the saturated salt-water is then pumped to the surface, and the salt recovered by evaporation. The fourth is lake-salt, which comes from saline lakes and is processed the same way as sea-salt.

A CRIMSON LAKE.

Approaching the site at Lake Grassmere was like wandering on to the aftermath of a nuclear accident. Everything was bleached out, there were huge salt mountains and dry wastelands of pink, blue, turquoise and white ponds as far as the eye could see. The vision was not dissimilar to the thermal lakes at Wai-o-tapu but without the steam and there wasn't even one dress shop. Even the huge machinery is eerily bleached, and by the end of the shoot we had the taste of salt in our throats just from breathing. Almost every grain of salt in New Zealand — 65,000 tons of it — starts at Dominion Solar Salt Works. Sea water is pumped through more than a dozen lakes that slowly evaporate the water. Three years later, it ends up at the coloured crystallising ponds where it is ten times more concentrated than when it started out. It is so saturated with salt, it simply drops to form a bed at the bottom of the pond. Drain the pond and harvest your salt.

I was admiring the beauty of the pink pond (the pink colour is due to an algae) against the blue sky, when they made me walk the plank. I had to walk out along the length of a narrow plank into the middle of an oedema-inducing saline lake. Just looking at it made my ankles swell. Then I had to do a piece to camera.

'Peta, could you take three steps back please?' requested camera-Chris.

'Very funny.'

'I think you should jump in this lake here and emerge slowly, so we can film the contrast between the pink and your red hair,' suggested sound-Chris.

'Don't worry,' said chief-Chris, 'it's only salt — you'd float. We'll brush you down after.'

'I want to go to the toilet.'

'You're no fun,' said sound-Chris.

On a hot day, forty tonnes of seawater are pumped into the lakes every minute, and that doesn't even equal the amount of water lost by evaporation in that very same minute. The

A MOUNTAIN OF SALT.

obvious question that came to mind here was — what if it rains? Rain is lighter than brine so it stays on the top and is decanted off, but persistent and heavy rain can be very damaging to the salt crust. We trailed into the processing and packaging plant past huge white-encrusted machines resembling dinosaurs caught in a frozen ice age. I kept expecting it to be cold.

Not many people know this, but salt has lots of other uses apart from domestic; only a small percentage ends up in our kitchens. The largest amount is used industrially by the freezing industry for treatment of hides and skins. It's also used in food processing, dye works, pharmaceuticals, water treatment, the paper industry and to make sausage skins, butter and cheese. Coarse, crystallised salt is also compressed into blocks to administer to farm stock in sodium-deficient areas.

Our last shoot for Marlborough was an interview with Piero for which he and Laurence had prepared a complement of regional products. Piero had lit the fire and waxed poetic for the camera about how he was living in a paradise of natural, pure food, perfect climate and great wine.

'Peta,' he stressed over and over again, 'you have a-to impress on people how important it is, the marriage between a-food and wine. One cannot go without the other. This is the future of a-New Zealand.' The *antipasto* (without pasta) platter was laden with Piero's Venetian Mussels, smoked salmon wrapped around lemon wedges, wood-roasted salmon, stuffed mussels, garlic dip, *Tapenade*, garlic bread, *ciabatta* bread and *grissini* (bread sticks).

MUSSELS STUFFED WITH *PROSCIUTTO* AND GARLIC

30 MUSSELS, CLEANED AND DEBEARDED

A LITTLE WHITE WINE

1/2 cup FRESH BREADCRUMBS

1/2 cup GRATED CHEESE

1/2 cup CHOPPED PROSCIUTTO HAM

1/2 cup CHOPPED PARSLEY

4 CLOVES GARLIC, CHOPPED

OLIVE OIL

GRATED PARMESAN CHEESE

Cook mussels in a covered pot with a little wine on high heat till they've opened. Remove the empty half shells and discard. Mix together the breadcrumbs, cheese, *prosciutto*, parsley and garlic in a bowl. Place the mussels in their shells on a tray and sprinkle a small amount of the mixture on each. Drizzle over a little oil, sprinkle on some Parmesan and grill under a high heat for a few minutes until golden and crispy.

PIERO'S VENETIAN MUSSELS

3 tbsp OLIVE OIL

2 ONIONS, PEELED AND SLICED IN ROUNDS

3 CLOVES GARLIC, CHOPPED

40 MUSSELS, WASHED AND DEBEARDED

1 cup DRY WHITE WINE

SALT AND FRESHLY GROUND PEPPER

1 cup CHOPPED PARSLEY

Heat the olive oil in a large fry-pan and sweat the onions and garlic for about ten minutes till soft. Throw in the mussels, wine, a little salt and lots of pepper. Cook over high heat till the mussels have opened, add the parsley and serve with lots of bread (preferably toasted on the remains of a fire) to soak up the juices.

GARLIC DIP

56 g TIN OF ANCHOVIES

8 CLOVES OF GARLIC, PEELED

2 SHALLOTS, PEELED

2 tbsp BALSAMIC VINEGAR

1 cup OLIVE OIL

Wash and drain the anchovies and place them in the blender along with the garlic, shallots and vinegar. Turn the machine on and drizzle the oil in till it makes a thick consistency. This dip is divine with seafood, but would, in my opinion, go equally well with steak or simply spread on crackers.

TAPENADE

Being very reticent people, the Ponders told me they made the best *tapenade* ever. I don't have their recipe but here's mine.

2 tbsp CAPERS
56 g TIN ANCHOVIES
1 tsp FRESH THYME
1 tbsp RUM OR COGNAC
2 tbsp OLIVE OIL OR MORE IF NEEDED
2 cups BLACK OLIVES
FRESHLY GROUND BLACK PEPPER

Throw the whole lot in the blender and process till the consistency you desire. Some people make a smooth paste of it, but I prefer it to be coarse. Some *provençal* cookbooks add tinned tuna, Dijon mustard, hard-boiled eggs, balsamic vinegar and a variety of other herbs like chervil and basil. In France this concoction is so loved, it is often served as an entrée with a fork to be eaten *comme ça*.

Balsamic (meaning healing or soothing) vinegar is a condiment much talked about and little understood. It has suddenly become fashionable, but beware, like olive oil it comes in varying qualities, so how do you know which one to buy? How do you know what you should be paying? A fortune is the short answer. If you didn't pay much for it, then it isn't the real thing. Balsamic vinegar is made like a *première cru* wine — it is the result of high-quality grapes, long, careful ageing and highly skilled craftsmanship. The older the vinegar and therefore the more concentrated the flavour, the higher the price. Balsamic vinegar or *aceto balsamico* comes from Modena in the Emilia-Romagna region of Italy and is considered to have medicinal properties. It has been around for centuries but has only become commercially available in the last thirty years. Before that you could only get hold of it as a gift.

Modena has the perfect climate and geography for the production of 'balsamico' — long, hot, dry summers for uninterrupted fermentation and cold winters for the important rest period. NOT UNLIKE MARLBOROUGH! I hereby challenge Piero to start making some balsamic vinegar. Barbara will kill me — he's already taken over their garage with his hams. In Italy the vinegar barrels are kept at the top of the house in a little room under the eaves. The barrel is *never* thrown out, any leaks being encased in wood. White sugary grapes are used, harvested as late as possible, crushed and stored in vats. At the first tremor of fermentation the must is cooked at 60–80°C, killing any yeast and sterilising. The liquid is then poured into a cask and a 'vinegar mother' added. The barrels are topped up with the must and left for twelve to fifty years.

A good balsamic vinegar should be dark brown to black and almost syrupy in consistency. Tasting fruity and sweet but with a balance of acidity and a complex, penetratingly aromatic smell, it only needs to be used in small amounts. If you want the real McCoy the bottle must read *'Tradizionale Aceto Balsamico di Modena'*. At a recent tasting in London, the show was stolen by a Modena vinegar costing a gob-smacking £115 for 10 centilitres! My theory is that the people who buy this vinegar are foodie bachelors who don't have wives that scream, 'You paid *what*? Don't worry about little Jimmy's schooling — he'll be *fine*, and as for my fantasies about having a new couch . . .' But should you develop a taste for balsamico and tatty couches, here's how you can enjoy yourself — use it to dress strawberries, transform a Bloody Mary, deglaze pan juices, jazz up a salad dressing or make it into a summer drink diluted with ice and sugar.

When the shoot had finished, the Chrises had to go off and do some 'pretties' so we prepared to say our goodbyes.

'What? You're not a-leaving me to eat all this food on my own,' said Piero, spreading his hands in supplication.

'Yes, it's for you and your staff,' said Laurence, 'we've got more work to do.'

'Well, you'll just have a-to come back. I've prepared a little snack for you and there's this a-bottle of 1994 Grove Hill Merlot . . .'

'Piero . . .'

'It's a-the winemaker's reserve . . .'

We all looked at each other.

'We'll be back.'

Upon our return a few hours later, we sat down to another memorable feast joined by Piero and Barbara. He had cooked a whole salmon *a l'étuvée*. Strictly speaking, this term means to braise, but it is really a more specific technique hardly ever used these days,

in which a dish is put under the oven or in the warming oven while other things are cooking so that it cooks very slowly by reflected heat. This is how Piero had cooked the salmon. It had sat on the bottom shelf of the salamander for a few hours. Other things were cooked, the heat was turned off, turned on again, life went on and still the salmon sat there. The result was a meal of indescribable succulence and voluptuousness topped off at the table with a sauce of garlic, parsley and olive oil. A 1995 Ponder Estate Chardonnay arrived followed by a 1990 Cloudy Bay Chardonnay. For dessert we dipped *biscotti* into little glasses of 1994 Highfield Noble Late Harvest. Someone said,

'Wouldn't you rather be doing the golliwogs or the cars?'

'NOT,' we all yelled, clinking our glasses with gusto.

We asked what we owed for the meal and of course there was no question of paying. I asked Piero if I could buy a whole *prosciutto* ham from him.

'You can have one but you can't pay for it,' he smiled.

'Oh yes, yes, yes, I insist on paying for it,' I said.

'I don't sell them.'

'Then I won't take one.'

'Take it. I want you to have it, Peta. In exchange you have to spread my message to the world about Marlborough.'

Dear reader I'm still eating it.

There are people in Marlborough who will make a lot of money but they will never have the happiness, love and *joi de vivre* of the Roccos. It depends what you call wealth, I suppose. They understand about 'the debt to pleasure', to steal from John Lanchester.

wellington

la table est le seul endroit ou l'on ne s'ennuie jamais pendant la première heure — the table is the only place where one never gets bored during the first hour

BRILLAT-SAVARIN

We filmed the Blenheim and Wellington segments back to back so jumped on the slinky *Lynx* to cross the channel. It was very smooth and the service very flash — just like being in a plane with flight attendants and everything. It was difficult to choose what our focus would be in Wellington because it's such a wonderful city and so much is going on there not only in terms of arts and theatre but also in terms of good food. Like any city, there are duds, and the last time I had been there I inexplicably found myself once again at a certain downtown restaurant. I had been speaking at the university orientation week. What does a person like me have to say to students — run now while you can — the best education is travel — the only reason I live in Auckland is because they won't let me into outer Mongolia? I was terrified of them but they didn't even throw one bun at me, I suppose because they were newies. By next year some of them could even be dealing coke in the dining-room. Afterwards, I wandered downtown in search of sustenance.

I settled into a table at this restaurant and waited. Silly me. I was one of three people in the place, there was a ratio of two staff per customer and the service was nonexistent. It wasn't that the staff were rude or dismissive, on the contrary they were very nice. It was that they just didn't appear to be there to serve, they were there for some other mysterious reason. They looked at me, saw that I needed something, saw that I was attracting their attention and pleasantly ignored me. I looked around and saw that it was the same story with the other customers. I had to beg for a menu, I had to get up and beg for pepper and salt, I had to get up and beg for coffee. The *antipasto* was a dry mixture of yellow cauliflower, acrid mushrooms, dry bread with no butter or oil and smoked salmon that looked like it had been shredded by a carrot peeler. This all happened last time I was here, but one likes to think it was an exception — it was depressing. I hadn't been so depressed since Bruce Springsteen married that blonde stick insect.

The next day I went back to the tried and true department at Boulcott Street. The Boulcott Street Bistro is a virtuoso bistro, a racehorse of a bistro, a real peak practice. I sat down at a crisply linened table and felt safe. The wait persons wore black waistcoats, long white aprons and black ties. I was served by a fine figure of a man possessed of a long mane of red hair tied back and a deep, gravelly voice. Call me old fashioned but I always think a tall man with a deep voice just guarantees a serious lunch. There were divine things on the menu like Bobby Calf Liver with Bacon and Braised Lettuce, Chicken *Boudin Blanc* with Pumpkin *Risotto*, *Confit* of Tuna with *Piperade* and Fillet *Béarnaise* with *Pommes Frites*. These mains only cost $21 on average and they were the real thing! Hundreds of fraudulent restaurants charge these prices for rubbish and most of them are on Ponsonby Road.

I ordered the Chicken *Boudin* and applied myself to my newspaper with startling results. The first headline I saw on the front page was BLOW-UP SHEEP — WHAT HAVE SEX SHOPS COME TO? I quickly opened up the paper and on page nine was a photograph of a woman in a satin blouse hiding behind a plastic blow-up pig. The article said that the blow-up sheep are designed for the rural Australian market. Who was it who told me Australia is a place where the men are men and the sheep are nervous? The *Boudin* arrived and was divine as I expected *and* there was Malden sea-salt on the table *and* a pepper grinder *per table*, not some ridiculous waiter standing over you with what looks like a didgeridoo grinding what one would be forgiven for thinking were diamonds, a habit I find too stupid and suburban for words.

I blanched and asked the redhead about this interesting sheep market, but he admitted he was not an expert. The article attempted to make fun of men by suggesting that realism was not uppermost in their minds. When is it, I asked myself? Did I say there was no sex in New Zealand? I lied. It's here and it's alive in Wellington. The dessert menu arrived suggesting things like *Sauternes* and Olive-Oil Cake with Poached Peach and *Crème Brûlée*, delicacies I managed to resist in the interests of getting my thighs off the chair. The service from beginning to end from the gorgeous redhead and everyone else was impeccable and warm hearted.

Wellington can also boast of dozens of Italian restaurants. Growing, catching or preparing food has always been a favourite way to make a living for Italians, and there is still a large Italian population in Wellington based in Island Bay, so Chris decided to 'do the Italians' for our Wellington segment. Despite Wellington's none-too-warm weather, it has always attracted immigrants from the warmer parts of Europe. Mostly the Italians came from the island of Stromboli near Sicily and Massalubrense in the Bay of Naples. They were workers of the land, peasant people and fishermen who, like so many others, had come in search of a better life. Stromboli is that rugged, volcanic island from the wonderful 1950 Ingrid Bergman film directed by Roberto Rossellini, where she falls in love with a poor fisherman. Of course, it all ended in tears but never mind. Looking at photos of the beautiful fishing villages where they made wine, pressed olives for oil, baked bread, grew capers, oranges and lemons, you wonder why they left. Their life in the new country was certainly tough. One of the first couples to make it to Wellington was Luigi and Isola Falleni who arrived in 1877. Isola was pregnant twenty-two times and gave birth to nineteen children, all of them at home and without medical assistance. The chilly, treacherous Cook Strait was hardly the Mediterranean, but the crayfish were abundant and there was a living to be made.

Like the earlier Bohemian immigrants at Puhoi, they faced great hardship and also, during the war, terrible prejudice and intern-ment. This was one of the saddest chapters of Italian history in New Zealand — men were interned for up to five years on Somes Island. This shameful episode caused enormous hardship and bitterness amongst the hard-working, patriotic Italian families. They couldn't understand how their men, some of whom were born here and most of whom were naturalised, could be considered enemy aliens.

Italians have green fingers. If they can find a space to grow something they will, even if it's only on the windowsill. Everybody had gardens full of tomatoes, zucchinis, grapes and herbs. Immigrants from Venice, Tuscany and the Dolomites started up market gardening in the Hutt Valley in the late 1920s and 1930s. Most of the hundreds of acres under cultivation are now under housing, but a few corners are still left. In the old days people used to bring their own fish to the chippie in Island Bay for him to cook, but these days there is just a handful of boats where once there were dozens.

There's little left to be seen of what was once little Italy, but behind a handful of suburban front doors, Italian tradition still lives on. The origins of Italian cooking are Greek, Roman and to a lesser extent Byzantine and oriental. The erudite Roman noble and gourmet Marcus Apicius, who led a completely dissolute life, committed suicide at age fifty-five rather than be forced to curtail his drinking and eating habits. In the fifteenth century the Venetians controlled the spice and sugar trade from India to Europe, which accounts for the Italians' love of herbs and spices in their cooking.

We had been encouraged by Caterina de Nave to contact Grace

Toscano, a wonderful old lady in Island Bay, if we wished to get a real tomato sauce. Grace came to Island Bay from Stromboli in the 1920s when she was ten. During the war, Italians were not allowed to live in a house by the sea 'in case we signalled the enemy', weren't permitted to listen to the radio at night and were spot checked by the police at any time. Grace remembers the terrible day when the family was having dinner one night and the police arrived to take away her brothers: 'We had been living here for years but we had

GRACE TOSCANO.

become the enemy.' She had a hard life but you can't see it in her pretty face, snowy hair and sparkling, black eyes. We arrived at the perfect little blue-and-white house with manicured lawns, to find dear Grace all dressed up and ready to go with her son and daughter in attendance. Grace can't really understand why people keep coming to film her and put her picture in the paper. She's a humble person who doesn't necessarily like attracting attention to herself. We had a lot in common.

We went into her vegetable garden, which took up the entire backyard. It was full of tomatoes, strawberries, zucchini, herbs, grapes, peppers, silver beet, beans and artichokes. Most of the garden was enclosed in shelters to protect it from the wind, and a fig tree was encased in a little house so it wouldn't grow too big. Grace makes her famous tomato sauce in the most simple way imaginable, the secret of the sweet taste being the acid-free tomatoes that come straight from her garden. The seeds from Italy were given donkey's years ago to her husband and even now she supplies half the neighbourhood with her sauce. She makes enough in the summer to keep her going all year. All she does is boil the whole tomatoes till they're mush, then purée them with a hand moulie and that's it!

The key is to grow or buy the beautiful, crimson, fleshy, acid-free tomato. I don't know why they are more expensive than other tomatoes because they are easy to grow. Grace made us her aubergine sandwich and the sauce that topped it was simply fried tomatoes — sweet and salubrious.

MULGIENE ALLA PARMIGIANA

GRACE TOSCANO'S AUBERGINE SANDWICH

2 LARGE AUBERGINES (EGGPLANTS)
SALT
500 g ACID-FREE TOMATOES
OLIVE OIL
1 cup FRESH BREADCRUMBS
1/2 cup CHOPPED PARSLEY
A FEW SPRIGS OF FRESH THYME
FRESHLY GRATED PARMESAN CHEESE
1 EGG
FRESHLY GROUND BLACK PEPPER

Peel the aubergines and slice lengthwise, about a centimetre thick. Sprinkle with salt and leave for half an hour to degorge the bitter juices. Cut the tomatoes in big chunks and fry in olive oil till soft.

Make the stuffing by combining the bread, herbs, a little Parmesan, the egg and salt and pepper in a bowl.

Wipe the aubergines dry then make sandwiches out of them with the stuffing. Heat lots of olive oil in a heavy fry-pan and fry the sandwiches on each side till golden and soft. It doesn't take long — about five minutes on each side.

To serve, lay out on a platter, cover with the fried tomatoes and sprinkle with lots of Parmesan.

Grace said that this sandwich can also be stuffed with sliced Mozzarella if you prefer, but she finds that too rich. I cooked this dish when I got home and it was surprisingly firm to the bite with the real, delicate flavour of the aubergine coming through. To go with this meal, Laurence put together a simple salad.

TOMATO AND BASIL SALAD

2 SLICES OF COUNTRY-STYLE BREAD FOR CROUTONS
OLIVE OIL
56 g TIN ANCHOVIES
500 g ACID-FREE TOMATOES
½ cup SUN-DRIED TOMATOES
BUNCH FRESH BASIL
BALSAMIC VINEGAR

Cube the bread and fry in oil till golden and crispy. Drain, wash and chop anchovies. Slice tomatoes, chop sun-dried tomatoes and chop basil. Place all this in a salad bowl and toss gently with a little vinegar and lots of oil.

After the shoot, Grace and her children made us tea served in the best flowery china with some of her *Cosi Dolci* (something sweet) — S-shaped cookies.

In the afternoon we went over to Nunzio di Gregorio's place to get on down and boogie with some real, home-made pizza. Nunzio is one of the last fishermen, making his living the old, traditional way. One day he decided he would like to be able to cook his own pizzas in his own backyard in his own wood-fired oven. When we turned up, his family were visiting from Italy and the men threw themselves into cooking. The wood-fired oven made by him and his friends, originally in the backyard, had become an extension of the house by the addition of a roof leading from the house to the oven. Now there was a large patio with flowers on the wall, plants, a fish pond, table and chairs and lights. The rest of the backyard was, of course, full of vegetables, crayfishing nets and sunshine. All we needed was an accordion, but we did have lots of help, smiling family and Italian red wine.

Nunzio's wife Frances told me her mother always makes Mozzarella and even today all Italian households make their

SETTING UP TO INTERVIEW NUNZIO DI GREGORIO.

own. The huge, pale Mozzarellas lay on the table like truncheons, and when Nunzio told me the cheese making was woman's work, my eyes opened very wide. We agreed that we wouldn't get into a discussion about what was woman's work and what wasn't. Frances tried to explain to me how to make Mozzarella, but I got lost somewhere between the three tonnes of milk and the burning of the fingers when you work the cheese. It's a lot of work and uses a lot of milk so that's why it's expensive to buy. The best is *Di Nora Bocconcini*, distributed by Kapiti cheeses.

HOME-MADE MOZZARELLA.

Real Italian pizzas are very thin and have very little topping. You cut a triangle, fold it over and eat it. Nunzio and his visiting relatives made enough pizzas for Africa and I assume they are still feeding the rest of the neighbourhood. Some had home-made tomato sauce as a base and some had freshly peeled and chopped acid-free tomatoes. On top of that went a little basil, some thyme and thin slices of Mozzarella. Simple and fresh is best according to Nunzio. *Saporita!*

Italians have always cooked with flair and style, begging you to share their passionate understanding and love of good food, none more so than the famous Remiro Bresolin of Il Casino restaurant on Tory Street in downtown Wellington.

Remiro is from Blessaglia di Pramaggiore near Portogruaro, thirty kilometres from Venice. On finishing military service, he and his friends set off for excitement, adventure and romance. Via Mexico he ended up in London and fell in love with his English teacher whom he followed back to New Zealand in 1973. Remiro's degree was in art, so he taught art and Italian in Auckland and travelled around New Zealand in his spare time. While visiting Wellington he got involved in a great idea with some friends — why not open a pizza joint?

Whether for religious reasons or through sheer ignorance — we shall never know — there were no pizzas in those dark days, so people had to survive on pies and chips. The idea of cooking food quickly so you could still identify it at the end was unheard of in this era. My mother put the steak on at 5 pm, went away and weeded the garden for an hour, then served shoe leather for dinner. We thought it was fabulous and every night my darling father said, 'My dear, you have excelled yourself.'

Remiro and his friends imported pizza ovens, espresso machines and Italian wine from Australia. I remember the first espresso machines in Auckland. They were considered to be a threat to national security not to mention morals. Honestly, I don't know how we survived the Dalmatians and the Italians. If it wasn't for them and their fancy continental ideas, we would still be happily drinking milk with the roast.

Anyway, Remiro was not only a good pizza maker, he had a magnetic personality. Like all people with big personalities, some people hate you and some people love you, and like most Italians Remiro has an explosive temperament. But I am getting ahead. To continue the story, Wellingtonians went mad over these pizzas and lined up in their thousands to eat them. The Wellington Special cost $1.20. More pizza shops were opened, partners came and went and in 1978 Remiro bought Il Casino.

It started off small and gradually he bought the rest of the building, turning Il Casino into a huge upstairs-downstairs palace with different flavoured rooms. In the brochure the restaurant is described rather floridly thus: 'The soul of Italy in the heart of Wellington. This is not a restaurant, it's life. *La vita Italiana*. Here are dark corners for shared secrets and whispered intimacies, rich salons for the grand gesture, *la conversazione animata, l'affare importante*. Blue jeans and Chanel. A flash of gold and the laughter of children. Sunlight and shadow. The smell of yeast, oregano, *parmeggiano* and fresh summer herbs. A splash of red on a starched white cloth. A synthesis in fact.' Whew!

The outside wall has a mural of Venice painted on it, and it was in front of this wall I battled with the wind to say my piece to camera. I was eventually allowed into the hallowed halls to meet Remiro, a tall, slim, suave man in a sharply cut suit. He had a very urbane air about him with his longish hair combed straight back and was every inch *la bella figura*. He was in the *Pizzeria*, making imaginary pizzas for the camera. It was Sunday and we had the place to ourselves. The outdoor *Pizzeria* had a large wood-fired oven, wooden tables, tiles embedded in the concrete floor and busts and sculptures scattered about. On the way back into the restaurant you walk through the terrace, which was dressed in white tablecloths, steel chairs, white marble floors, trellises and fans.

While Remiro made us espressos as only an expert can, with just the right amount of warmth and a perfect crema, I wandered into the kitchen to meet the chef, Franco Zanotto. Franco is Remiro's brother-in-law, whom Remiro maintains he tricked into coming to New Zealand to run his kitchen. He is a master chef of the old Venetian school, disciplined, ordered and a refined cook. *L'anima della tradizione. L'anima della cucina.* It was the Venetians who introduced forks and glasses to the table. In 1533 Catherine de Medici married the Dauphin (who became King Henry II of France), brought her Venetian chefs with her and that's how the French learned to cook. The French refined what they learned from the Italians, but the everyday people in Italy weren't affected by the Frenchification of their cuisine and to this day Italian food has remained largely localised and traditional.

The large, double kitchen was clean beyond description, a realm of harmony and lucidity. Having worked in many restaurant kitchens, I know exactly what they look like under the surface because the last thing you feel like doing after a hard night is spending another hour cleaning. I checked everywhere — under the benches, on high shelves, inside ovens — everything was spotless. Shiny copper pots hung over the stoves, there were huge skylights and all the equipment was lined up in neat piles. Franco is a bearded man with glasses who is as quiet as Remiro is loquacious. With us he was gentle, pleasant but serious and very patient. How he is with his nine kitchen staff, I have no idea, but we all know what chefs are really like — crazy people. The biggest tantrums I have ever thrown in my life have been in kitchens.

Upstairs there was more dining space and a piano bar where you can hang out till the small hours exchanging fashion hints and telling stories about the one that got away. Some people also talk about fishing. Don't think that was the end of the story because there was yet another room called *Casa Battelli*, a splendid private room with panelled walls and roaring log fire for that intimate little *je ne sais quoi.*

Franco's specialty is the cooking of the north — *Tripa Parmeggiana, Gnocchi Verdi, Fegato alla Venezia, Risotto.* He made us a meltingly good Venetian rabbit dish called *Coniglio in Humido,* which we got to eat at the end of the shoot. This dish has been entered into the Corban's Food and Wine Challenge this year. I'm very partial to bunny and lots of supermarkets have them now. Get the butcher to portion the meat for you and you will not be disappointed in the tender, low-fat flavour of rabbit.

FRANCO'S CONIGLIO IN HUMIDO

1 *WHOLE RABBIT CUT INTO PORTIONS*

1 *cup* *DRY WHITE WINE*

OLIVE OIL

RIND OF 1 LEMON

½ cup CARROTS, DICED

½ cup CELERY, DICED

SALT AND FRESHLY GROUND PEPPER

1 *tsp FRESH SAGE*

1 *tsp WHOLE CLOVES*

1 *ONION, CHOPPED*

1 *RED PEPPER, SLICED*

1 *cup DRIED PORCINI MUSHROOMS*

1 *cup FAGIOLI (FRESH BORLOTTI BEANS) — IF UNAVAILABLE USE BROAD BEANS*

1 *cup TOMATO PUREE*

2 *SALSICCIE (ITALIAN PORK SAUSAGE), SLICED*

CHERRY TOMATOES FOR GARNISH

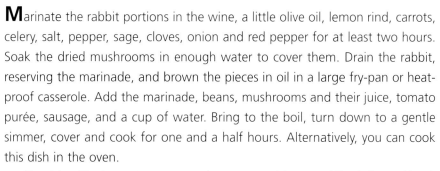

Marinate the rabbit portions in the wine, a little olive oil, lemon rind, carrots, celery, salt, pepper, sage, cloves, onion and red pepper for at least two hours. Soak the dried mushrooms in enough water to cover them. Drain the rabbit, reserving the marinade, and brown the pieces in oil in a large fry-pan or heat-proof casserole. Add the marinade, beans, mushrooms and their juice, tomato purée, sausage, and a cup of water. Bring to the boil, turn down to a gentle simmer, cover and cook for one and a half hours. Alternatively, you can cook this dish in the oven.

Garnish with cherry tomatoes and consume with a good Bardolino or Tocai.

Next Franco made a complicated little dessert called *Budino di Gélato*, which requires special equipment (on the part of the tools, not the chef) and precise measurements but is worth the effort. Basically you make a very thin sponge then line ramekins or small pastry rings with it, which you fill with *gélato*, *Sambucca* and *amoretti* biscuits. Franco makes them up in large numbers in a specially designed plastic container and bakes the sponge on an oven-proof, plastic sheet. They can be made in advance, kept in the freezer and taken out five minutes before serving.

BUDINO DI GELATO

SPONGE BOXES FILLED WITH *GÉLATO*

FOR THE SPONGE:

125 g (APPROX 2) EGGS

90 g SUGAR

90 g FLOUR

Beat the eggs and sugar together till white, then add the flour.

160 g (APPROX 3) EGG WHITES

30 g SUGAR

30 g MELTED BUTTER

Beat egg whites till stiff and add sugar. Fold the two mixtures together, adding the butter.

TO MAKE THE *BUDINO*:

200 g ICING SUGAR

FEW DROPS OF FOOD COLOURING

GELATO OR ICE-CREAM

SAMBUCCA

100 g AMORETTI BISCUITS

COCOA

CONTINUED NEXT PAGE

FRANCO SHOWS PETA HOW TO MAKE *BODINO DI GÉLATO*.

Make an icing from icing sugar, a little water and some food colouring — whatever colour you like. Spread this thinly on a baking tray covered in baking paper and make wavy designs on it with a fork. When the icing has set, spread the sponge mixture thinly on top of it. Bake in a hot oven for five minutes. Allow to cool then invert the baking paper with the sponge on it so that the wavy icing side is now on top.

Cut slices of the sponge the height and circumference of your ramekins and line the ramekins or small pastry rings with them, making sure the icing is on the outside. Fill these up with *gélato* then sprinkle them with a little Sambucca. Scrunch the *amoretti* biscuits up with a little cocoa and sprinkle on top. Freeze for a few hours then carefully remove the 'boxes' from their containers. Franco served them to the starving crew with a plum *coulis* and chocolate crowns, which I was sorely tempted to use as hair decoration.

Remiro and I sat down for an interview in front of the rabbit dish with huge glasses of Pinot Grigio and great Italian arias on the CD in the sumptuous main dining-room.

We ignored the camera and talked in French about culture, Pavarotti, fashion (his wife Rosaria Hall has a glamorous dress shop in the same building as Il Casino, called Bresolini), and idiot useless Italian cooks who give Italian food a bad name. Remiro is a man of definite opinions, one of the most contrary being that Wellington has great weather. This blind chauvinism regarding Wellington I found rather charming. Some of his other opinions I can't repeat here if I ever wish to eat in his restaurant again, but I did hear some good stories about Il Casino from the mother of a friend who used to dine there years ago.

'Oh, Il Casino,' she said laughing, 'we've had some very good times in that place over the years. They started very small and the food has always been superb. They have remained traditional and have not been ruined by their success, but there've been lots of dramas there. They've been bombed; the owners had fights; all sorts of amazing people went there — *mafiosi*, diplomats, the international community, lots of Europeans. They never attracted the *nouveaux riches*; they were never vulgar; their customers were not all car salesmen like Aucklanders. We used to live in Vanuatu and we had meetings at Il Casino with the Belgian Ambassador. He asked us lots of questions and gave us a bottle of Belgian liqueur, which I still have. It turned out he was a spy. Yes, Il Casino always had class.'

At the end of the shoot, we hung around the fantastic, inlaid, Carrara-marble table at reception, enjoying a few more stories and a few more minutes of respite from the 'wonderful' weather outside. Then we hit it. I laughed in its face and instantly lost my hairdo, the

Chrises put their hands in their pockets to ground themselves and the cameras walked to the next location on their own. Our last stop before flying back to the throbbing metropolis of Auckland was the Italian festival at the Petone Settlers' Museum. By now it was not only windy but also suddenly cold and rainy. Brave tarantella dancers were trying not to slide into the break and the choir was holding on desperately to their music. I took one look and ran back to the car. On our way to the airport I had the awful thought, 'What if those poor women are still standing in the rain and wind singing, their words instantly snatched away to some secret place, certainly nowhere near the location of the festival?'

prétendre qu'il ne faut pas changer de vins est une hérésie; la langue se sature; et apres le troisième verre, le meilleur vin n'éveille plus qu'une sensation obtuse — to pretend that you must not change wines is heresy; the tongue saturates itself; and after the third glass, the best wine only arouses an obtuse sensation

BRILLAT-SAVARIN

napier

napier was another town I visited on my tour with the *Listener* Women's Book Festival. I liked it so much and found the standard of hospitality so above and beyond the call of duty, that I talked the *Town & Country* team into doing our Hawke's Bay segment there. On my way home from filming in Central Otago I did a couple of days' research in Napier. They say Hawke's Bay people are conservative, but under those westie haircuts (a lot of the men emulate Michael Law's coiffeur) and tightly buttoned white blouses lies seething passion and personal relationships with grapes. They make brutally difficult, extremely dangerous treks from one farm to another with nothing to sustain them but barbecued sheep's testicles and hip-flasks. Gentle reader, when it was suggested to me that I was just a city girl who could never fit into country life; 'not the sort to ever get my shoes dirty', I was wounded to the core. Did I not tramp into a potato field to dig spuds? Did I not leap unaided on to fishing boats? Did I not ride a horse along Omapere Beach? I rest my case.

My friends in Napier took me to a restaurant that was so bad I almost made a brutally difficult, extremely dangerous trek into the kitchen to express myself to the cook. I had asked to go somewhere cheap and cheerful and was taken to 'the little restaurant that dares to be different'. There were four of us. Two of us ordered only appetisers from a list featuring such artistry as Left Bank Chowder (a South Seas delicacy) and Chef's Salad (always fresh and zesty). Two of us ordered from the mains list featuring such brazen things as Neptune's Delight (I'll leave that to your imagination). Wait, no I can't. This dish was described as 'a selection from the Pacific with pastry fish'. I'm not making this up. This sentence closely rivalled the haggis sentence at the Queenstown Food and Wine festival. One conjured up images of pastry fish happily frolicking with frozen baby octopus in an underwater playground. I ordered a steak as there was simply nothing else that didn't scare me to death. Four mains were listed, then three desserts, then an advertisement for over-priced wines, then suddenly as a little trick to make sure you were awake, two more mains appeared.

It was obvious to anyone, no matter how intellectually challenged, that as that was all we had ordered, all the meals had to arrive at the same time. As soon as the waiter had sloped off to the kitchen I knew what would happen next — call it feminine intuition. I turned to my friend Alan and said:

'How much do you want to bet that you get your *entrées* first and we wait for our mains?'

'No. The waiter is surely not that stupid,' Alan replied, hunched over his beer.

'How much?'

'A pavlova.'

'I'll add a whisky to that,' said Kingsley. Had I known the mains would arrive forty-five minutes after the *entrées*, I would have committed hara-kiri immediately as neither pavlova nor well-done steak appeal to me. We waited and waited. There was one other table of customers in the restaurant. Still we waited. The thing about making people wait a long time for their food is that a variety of things can happen and everybody reacts according to their own character. Kingsley remained completely calm but with wary alertness should he need to deflect knives or anything, Randall started telling long, involved stories to distract us, I was slowly moving from incredulousness to clinical insanity and Alan thought it was hilarious.

'Peta,' he said, 'I can't believe you're taking this. I would have thought by now you would at least have swept the table top on to the floor. Now that you've got ten minutes on TV, suddenly you turn into a wimp.'

Kingsley got a look on his face that said 'please don't encourage her'.

At the point where I had been pushed beyond endurance and had almost talked the others into leaving, I underwent a psychological shift and decided to use the 'flip side' of the experience. My brother Jonathan taught me about the flip side. I have a spiritual tendency to assume every silver lining has a cloud lurking somewhere and he is the opposite.

'Peta,' he says, 'turn the coin over — there are always two ways of seeing a thing.'

'That sounds suspiciously like "trust in the universe",' I say.

'Don't go new age on me. You love exaggerating.'

The 'thing' was so ridiculous, I decided to enjoy it for what it was — a little bit of theatre on the stage of life. This improved attitude on my part did not, unfortunately, have any affect on the universe. The salad appeared to have been shredded by a gang of Rottweilers, the salad dressing tasted like the aftermath of an artificial insemination experiment and OF COURSE the steak was suitably inedible. Randall was moved to give the waiter a long, condescending, Oscar Wildeish lecture on the finer points of service, Kingsley's face was a study in controlled floor perusal and Alan gazed open mouthed at the waiter as I wrote it all down. The waiter registered polite disinterest and returned to the kitchen. One minute later loud screaming in a foreign language emanated from that area, which was the exact moment another customer rose to his full height, moved to the old piano and began playing. No one could have thought it up. I looked around for Woody Allen.

A few months later we travelled from rainy Auckland to sunny Napier for the *Town & Country* shoot. I was happy to be back in the Hawke's Bay in spite of 'unnamed of Hastings'. My friends in Havelock North assured me that no one cared what anyone in Hastings thought. It was approaching April Fool's day and people were recounting some of the stunts they had witnessed. The best April Fool jokes appear to come from the British, like the announcement on the radio that the next two Thursdays would be cancelled because Britain had lost two days since the war. People called in to ask if they had to pay their staff on those days. The most famous story was the one about spaghetti. English television featured a story about a spaghetti harvest in Switzerland, showing spaghetti hanging from trees. The villagers were seen carrying big baskets of newly harvested spaghetti to be dried in the sun. The switchboards were jammed with enquiries as to how you could grow spaghetti in your own backyard. Another good one was when the BBC told listeners that because Pluto would pass directly behind Jupiter on 1 April, a gravitational pull on the earth would make everyone feel lighter. People were told that if they jumped at a certain time, they would stay up longer than usual. Punters called in saying they had actually floated around the room.

On my reccie visit, I had spoken to Frenchman Gerard Flaschner and his New Zealand born wife Jacqueline of Mon Logis and it was here that we stayed during our filming.

Chris and Laurence arrived a day earlier than me to get our victims sorted. I got an open-armed welcome from the splendid Flaschners, she being just as beautiful and he being just as dapper with a twinkle in the eye. There was the smell of bread in the oven and perfume in the bedrooms. Jacqui got me settled in my room with the white cotton linen, feather duvets, iron bedsteads and terrace that looked out on to the beach. Mon Logis is a double-

MON LOGI.

storeyed, verandahed villa built in 1915, overlooking the Pacific breakers on Napier's Marine Parade. Jacqui and Gerard have made it into a private hotel in the French tradition. He does the cooking, specialising in *provençal* dishes and she does the cosseting, specialising in charm, personal service and style. The hotel is elegant and relaxing, breakfast is just about anything you want and dinner is *table d'hôte* meaning silver service, five courses and dining with the hosts.

Gerard made us a simple pasta dish with tomato and garlic for dinner followed by Puhoi cheeses and a chocolate mousse with a Muscat. He gave Laurence strict orders not to wear shorts and sandals to dinner.

'Gerard,' Jacqui admonished gently, 'you eat too quickly darling — you're finished already.'

'I eat quickly and drink slowly,' he replied with a sniff.

'This is sounding suspicious,' I said, ploughing into the cheese, 'I hope you don't do everything quickly Gerard.'

'No he doesn't,' Jacqui smiled.

Before retiring Gerard had to know exactly what we wanted for breakfast and at exactly what time. Jacqui wrote it all down on little cards. We all had to go into incredible details about the contents of the breakfast.

In the morning after a sleepless night thanks to three-million-tonne apple-trucks thundering by all night, I approached the breakfast table in a truculent mood. Chris and Laurence were already into it and chirping away. I had said the night before that I absolutely only wanted an *Omelette aux Herbes* — nothing else and it arrived thus. The minute I saw Chris's mushrooms and bacon, I wanted some. I broached the subject with Jacqui. A cloud passed over her beautiful brow.

'He won't like it,' she said.

My omelette was whipped away and returned with a few mushrooms on it. Laurence's arrived and he made a formal complaint about the distinct lack of mushrooms. Gerard mumbled and fussed from the kitchen. Jacqui smiled benignly.

'We weren't like this yesterday were we, Jacqui?' said sucky Laurence. 'We're only like this now that *she's* here. We were easy to feed before we met her.'

Obviously if we were in Napier we were going to talk wine. From time immemorial wine has had symbolic significance. In Greek mythology, Dionysus (the god of wine) associated wine with joy, happiness and high spirits, and Jesus chose wine to symbolise his blood, so strongly was it associated with spiritual values. Wine has a nobility that makes it the very symbol of family and social festivity. Baudelaire said, 'If the human race abandoned the production of wine, a void in human health and spirit would ensue, an absence more horrible than anything that the excesses of wine could ever lead to.'

Wine is an ancient form of therapy, both physiological and psychological. It is an anti-depressant along with chocolate; in fact, if you want to be happy and slim, live on a diet of red wine and dark chocolate. It is rich in vitamins and minerals, especially B3 which regenerates the liver and allows for the elimination of toxins. It contains phenolics, which are antioxidants — they're the ones that fight cellular damage and keep you young and beautiful for ever. Acidic white wines like Chardonnay and Champagne are diuretic, promoting the proper elimination of toxins. Aged wine has qualities as a bacteriocide, antiseptic and antihistamine. So now it's official — wine is good for you — a little bit of what you fancy does you good.

Working out at the gym and being in bed by ten o'clock is for losers, and believe me I feel bad about it.

Moderate wine drinkers live longer, get fewer colds, have a higher level of resistance to illness in general, have healthy hearts and can carry heavy boxes of wine long distances. In fact, research has shown that you're looking for trouble if you don't drink wine, especially red wine, especially aged, good red wine. We drink wine far too young in New Zealand so the medicinal effects are pretty minimal, I hate to tell you. In spite of their high-fat diet, the French have one-third the heart-attack rate of Americans. They are the biggest wine drinkers in the world. OK so they also eat a lot more fruits, vegetables and grains than anybody else but they sure understand how to live. It is the tannin in wine that contains the procyanidines that affect cholesterol, and if you can't say those words, you've already had too much to drink. The real message is moderation. If you drink too much it ruins your looks and your health, and if you don't drink at all you could end up being a social bore with clogged arteries. The most recent message from the Department of Health is two glasses of wine a day for men and one for women. The message from French doctors is no more than half a litre a day.

We drove off to the Sacred Hill winery to meet up with our Napier camera crew Richard Williams and his partner Barbara. A nine am appointment had been set up with David Mason, one of the brothers who own the winery, to film some hand-pressing at the Rockwood plant. This is a very unromantic outfit in the industrial zone, but the top of the range wines are still made up at the vineyard. We had been told about the Mason boys:

WITH DAVID MASON AT SACRED HILL.

'They're a bunch of artists . . .'

'The place runs on a system of organised chaos . . .'

'In the old days the winemaking was bloody rough — foot pressing, dirty bottles, wasps everywhere — absolute bloody nightmare . . .'

'The Masons are wonderful — you'll love them. They're old

Hawke's Bay, have a colourful history and know how to enjoy life . . .'

David wasn't there and the hand press wasn't even set up, let alone ready to go. In the world of television time is money and normally people are so thrilled that you are giving them all the free publicity, they fall over themselves to accommodate you, but this was Sacred Hill. The fact that we had a lot to get through that day was just too bad, so Richard started shooting the huge stainless-steel tanks. Presently, David wandered in smiling and relaxed and said to Richard,

'Just make sure you shoot the right bloody thing.'

'Yeah well, I'll have a hard time bloody making something out of this mate.'

David was tall with wild black hair, craggy eyebrows and eyes that looked like they'd endured a few wine-athons, a few Bacchanalian overdoses, a few vinous banquets. Laurence gave me a look that said 'just stick to the interviewing, kid'.

While we waited for the hand-press to be assembled, I looked around for some written information about Sacred Hill. David and Mark Mason got sick of paying ridiculous prices for a good glass of wine on their student incomes, so decided to make their own, or so the fable goes. In 1986 they used a little of the fruit from their father's contract vineyard. The Fumé Blanc they made was great, so they established Sacred Hill and now have three ranges. The first is the Reserve Sacred Hill range, the second is the Sacred Hill Whitecliff (for whites) and Dartmore (for reds), which is the staple range, and the third is the Rockwood range which is cheaper. This tier uses some grapes from Marlborough and it was at the Rockwood winery we now found ourselves.

MALBEC GRAPES IN THE HAND PRESS.

Certain grapes like 'Malbec', which are used for blending, are isolated to be hand-picked and hand-pressed because they are grown in small amounts. I emerged from the tearoom to see a small woman inside a big vat full of macerating grapes. She was bucketing them out into the now-assembled hand-press. When they were all in, Jenny emerged dressed in jeans, gumboots, a big plastic apron and wine-dark arms. She put the wooden lid on the press, held in place by blocks, and hand-cranked it down to squeeze out the juice. As the liquid ran out, Jenny tasted it frequently for floral, vegetal, chocolate and tannic traits.

'The harder you press the more the juice tastes of tannin,' she explained. 'You have to know when to stop pressing.'

Jenny and I got to have a little *parlez-vous*. I discovered that she had only recently come back to New Zealand from ten years in France as a winemaker. For many years she ran a vineyard in Bordeaux, where 'Malbec' comes from and is now employed as a red-wine consultant.

Just as we were about to leave, David announced that a truck full of 'Sauvignon Blanc' grapes was arriving and did Richard want to film it. He not only filmed it but the entire crew, except *moi*, wore it. They jumped up on the ledge to shoot the grapes being tipped into the receival bin for crushing and — *whoops* — almost drowned in a sea of grapes that did a spectacular back wash (which they swear was deliberate on the part of the truck operator). For the rest of the day they walked around picking sticky 'Sauvignon Blanc' grapes off themselves.

Next we drove up to Sacred Hill in the Dartmore Valley. The Hawke's Bay has been making wonderful wine for over a hundred years and has often been compared to the Bordeaux region. The Mission Vineyard was founded by the Catholic Society of Mary in 1851 and remains under the same management today. Te Mata Estate started in the 1870s and the McDonald Winery was built in the 1890s. This is big Chardonnay and Cabernet Sauvignon country. The Dartmore Valley is protected from coastal breezes by a range of hills. Lots of autumn heat gives the area a big advantage with the late-maturing varieties, but what's only recently been recognised is the extraordinary range of microclimates and soil types on offer. River gravels and calcareous silts from the surrounding limestone hills and river terraces provide this variety of fertility, and in recent years the focus for new plantings has moved inland to low-vigour areas around Hawke's Bay's rivers.

Sacred Hill is beside the Tutaekuri and Mangaone Rivers, and tiny corners of the vineyard have been identified for specific wine types. Their wines are interesting, different and idiosyncratic, just like themselves, and they're divergent — sometimes they're exceptional and sometimes they completely miss the boat. They make Cabernet/Merlot, Chardonnay reserve, Gewürztraminer late harvest, Pinot Noir, Sauvignon Blanc barrel fermented, Cabernet Rosé late harvest and Pinot Blanc. The winery itself is set amid spectacular scenery surrounded by gardens and trees and one can eat here, go fishing and swimming and play *pétanque*. The last time I was here I was reading from my first book for the *Listener* Women's Book Festival. It was raining, I had had no sleep and it was an outside do. As soon as I opened my mouth, I was given a glass of wine and the sun came out, so I've had a soft spot for Sacred Hill ever since.

The Sacred Hill winery is where the old-fashioned methods are still used, and because of all these different soils and microclimates, it's a bit like Burgundy where almost every row produces a different wine. David said good wine is going back to the vineyard now because everyone can produce high-tech standards in the processing. While he and Laurence played *boules*, Chris and Richard got a bench set up for an interview. Mark Mason wandered past and ignored us.

'Where's the wine?' I asked.

'Why aren't we in the vineyard?' David asked.

'Why am I the director?' Chris asked.

'I still think we should do this interview in the vineyard,' smiled David.

I got a ride down to the vineyard in David's beat up BMW that he had to stop periodically and stick a screwdriver into.

'Haven't got a clue what I'm doing,' he said to me over the hood, 'somebody told me to put the screwdriver in here if it made this noise. Works every time.'

We conducted our interview with me standing on a small rock to achieve eye level with David and chatted away to the accompaniment of bird guns going off constantly. He was very easy and articulate to interview and on the way back to the winery showed us his favourite G & T stop — a sheer cliff overlooking the riverbed. I could barely stand the danger *without* a gin.

In the late afternoon/early evening, we went to meet Clyde Potter of Epicurean Supplies. Napier/Hastings has been dubbed New Zealand's fruit bowl, the Mediterranean-style climate and rich soil being perfect for market gardening. Drive around and the number of fruit and vegetable stalls is mind boggling. Clyde grows organic herbs and vegetables specialising in produce that's a little different, then he trucks them overnight to chefs throughout the country. He grows wonderful things like baby vegetables, unusual herbs, borage flowers for salads, all kinds of fancy lettuce, golden beetroot, courgette flowers, rocket and elephant garlic.

The most dramatic thing about Epicurean Supplies was the method of weed control. With organically grown produce there are, of course, no sprays and lots of weeds, so Clyde has a scorched-earth policy, a purification by fire, a medieval flame thrower. He's got this torture machine that looks like a dreadful new way of increasing the productivity of workers. Chris wanted to film this bit at dusk to increase the visibility of the flames and to add to the eeriness of the scene. While I wandered off to pick walnuts from the huge tree out the back of the property (most people don't know what *fresh* walnuts taste like as what we buy in the shops are usually rancid), the others played boy games with the flame weeder. The weeder, which is pulled by a tractor, has four gas cylinders fuelling flames that shoot out from underneath. It passes slowly over rows of just barely showing weeds once a week for three weeks, burning the daylights out of any living thing. Then you plant out and don't see weeds for ages — it works remarkably well. The process is not unlike waxing your legs only it's more fun and weeds aren't actually being yanked out of your tender woman flesh.

That evening we had dinner at Pierre sur le Quai restaurant on West Quai, Ahuriri. Pierre Vuilleumier is a Swiss chef cooking French provincial-style food in a beautiful restaurant overlooking the fishing port. It has won an architectural award, and for the past two years was Michael Guy's regional restaurant of the year. Pierre and his New Zealand born wife Susan run the place like a European *bistro* in the sense that the kitchen is always open and customers are always welcome to drop in for a glass of wine, a coffee or just a chat. The three times I have been to Pierre's people have walked into the kitchen to talk, Pierre keeps working and everyone feels at home. Susan sometimes feeds the kids there, and the food is prepared and cooked by someone who has a solid base and high standards in refined cooking. All sorts of people eat at Pierre's and there is no dress code — you do what you like and wear what you like. We ate wonderful things like Rabbit in Mustard Sauce with Pasta, Home-made Ravioli Stuffed with Duck, Fresh Tuna with Three Sauces, home-made bread and Seafood Ragout. The first time I ate there someone asked for Pierre's famous *Crème Brûlée* and there were no more left. At ten o'clock at night, Pierre turned around and made a batch *à la commande* and burnt the tops with a blow torch. That's the kind of man he is.

the next morning at breakfast Gerard cooked me one of everything to keep me quiet. I sat sipping my fresh orange juice in the pale-green dining-room with the pink and yellow damask curtains and French cherrywood furniture, feeling quite happy. I put on a little pink blouse and black satin skirt (people are now starting to complain that I look too straight) and tripped off to investigate that medicinal fruit that begins being harvested on Valentine's Day and keeps the doctor away.

Napier is fruit, fruit, fruit, apples, apples, apples. Hawke's Bay's hot days and cool nights are just what apples like because it loads them up with sugar. There's no such thing as a bad apple here, in fact they're big business. By the end of April, sixteen million cartons of apples will have been dispatched to some of the world's most high-profile buyers and at least two million of them roared past my bedroom at Mon Logis. At Philip Alison's orchard alone, 300,000

INTERVIEWING PHILLIP ALISON.

apples are picked every day. Most overseas markets require what amounts to a perfect-looking apple, and millions of dollars have been sunk into creating and packaging this beast, then weeding out the ones that don't quite pass the test.

Philip and his family live in the middle of the orchards in a wonderful ochre and azure house surrounded by roses. As usual Chris got me doing something idiotic. I took one look at the hydralada, didn't bother to ask what he had in mind and climbed into it. This is what the pickers hoist themselves up with to pick the apples and it's terrific fun. Once I'd figured out up and down, as opposed to backwards and forwards, the crew relaxed. Richard kept saying 'do it again' for absolutely no reason save personal entertainment. There were rows and rows of red and green trees, fecund and laden, bursting with luscious red fruit. The apple trees are not high and they're shaped like many tiered umbrellas.

Philip explained that each variety has a quite definite harvesting season of four weeks, and all the fruit of that variety has to be picked during that period. The 'Coxes' ripen first, then come the 'Galas'. By late March it's the turn of the 'Braeburns', then the 'Fujis' and finally the 'Granny Smiths'. Philip also grows 'Pacific Rose', which has a twin sister called 'Southern Snap', a 'Gala' and 'Splendour' cross. The crunchy 'Braeburn' is my favourite, but 'Royal Galas' are the biggest seller. The whole world loves them and everyone wants to grow them but no one has been able to match the Hawke's Bay taste. In New Zealand there is very intensive searching for new varieties and three have been developed in the last ten years, a very unusual feat. Apples like 'Red Delicious' and 'Granny Smith' are now considered old fashioned. There's more to an apple than its colour — each apple tastes different. Some are acid, some are very sweet, some are good for cooking. The big question is, with this huge export market, do we in New Zealand ever get to taste the best? Philip assured me at the beginning of the season we do and at any time of the year we definitely have a much superior product to anything growers overseas produce.

We grabbed a case of 'Braeburns' for our afternoon cooking class *chez* Gerard, and marched fearlessly into his kitchen. He had agreed to demonstrate his cold vegetable terrine and an apple tart. When my friends saw this segment on TV they all said, 'We thought you two were going to slap each other.' What happens when you put the two bossiest people in the world in the same kitchen? Fun. That's what. Gerard is your typical bombastic, impatient but funny Frenchman and I, of course, am all sweetness and light and always do what I'm told. We set up the essentials — Pernod, water, ice and glasses and spent the next two hours indulging in a bilingual slinging match.

'*Bon*, Peta. First of all you throw all the pastry ingredients in the blender *d'accord*?'

'*Non*. I always make pastry with my hands.'

'*Mais* this is 1996.'

'I'm an old-fashioned girl.'

'*Enfin. Fait comme tu veux*,' (raising eyes to heaven).

'Gerard, this is incredibly gloopy, in fact it's a *bordel*. I've never made pastry like this.'

PETA AND GERARD DISCUSS THE *TARTE AUX POMMES*.

'If you had made it in the blender as I asked, you would have had no problem.'

I managed to get the pastry into a ball with the help of lots of flour, rolled it out, rolled it around the roller and laid it in the tart dish.

'You put it in the dish from left to right, *ma chère*,' he said.

'*Evidement!* You said that because I have just put it in from right to left,' I snapped.

'Have another Pernod and fan the apples out *comme ça* into the tart and on the top make a little flower.'

'*Santé*. Do you like my little flower, Gerard? It's not unlike yourself, dare I say it — a rare flower.'

'*Oui oui, ça va*. It's a long time since I was a little flower, *ma grande*.'

While all this was going on, Gerard also made his vegetable-and-herb aspic terrine called *Marché de Provence*, a perfect summer meal full of *provençal* vegetables like capsicums, thyme, courgettes and tomatoes.

MARCHE DE PROVENCE DE GERARD

GERARD'S VEGETABLES IN ASPIC

2 sachets OF GELATINE
1/2 litre OF VEGETABLE STOCK
1 EGGPLANT
2 COURGETTES
3 CAPSICUMS, GREEN, RED AND YELLOW
2 TOMATOES
OLIVE OIL
SALT AND FRESHLY GROUND PEPPER
FRESH THYME

Make the aspic by mixing the gelatine with the vegetable stock. Let it cool. Wash the eggplant and courgettes and cut into squares. Wash and empty the capsicums and cut into squares. Peel the tomatoes by dipping them in boiling water, seed them and cut into squares. Heat the olive oil and sauté the vegetables separately, sprinkling them with salt, pepper and thyme. They should be just cooked. Pour 1 cm of aspic into a terrine and cool it in the fridge for half an hour. Fill the terrine with the vegetables, alternating them for art and beauty, then pour in the rest of the aspic and refrigerate for twelve hours. To serve, you can sit the terrine in a sink of very hot water for a few minutes, then up-end it on to a serving platter. Slice with a knife that has been dipped in hot water. I think this lovely dish would be good served with a spicy tomato *concassé* (chunky sauce) or a red capsicum purée.

TARTE AUX POMMES
APPLE TART

FOR THE PASTRY:
200 g FLOUR
100 g SOFT BUTTER
¹/₂ tsp SALT
25 g SUGAR
2 EGGS

FOR THE TART:
6 APPLES, PEELED, HALVED AND CORED
SUGAR
BUTTER
HONEY
CERAMIC PIE DISH

To make the pastry, put the flour, butter, salt and sugar into a blender and blend briefly. Add the eggs and blend till the pastry forms a ball (won't take long). Or put the flour on the bench and make a hole in the middle. Into this hole put the salt, sugar and butter. Blend with your fingertips, gradually drawing in all the flour. Next add the eggs, make a big mess and form the pastry into a ball with the help of flour. Don't wear rings while doing this as they will end up in the rubbish when you try to get all the paste off your hands. Leave the pastry to rest for half an hour while you recover with a Pernod and slice up the apples.

'Braeburn' apples are really good for tarts because they hold their shape and are nice and tart if you'll pardon the pun. Lay the apple halves flat on the bench and slice them very thinly. Chop the end bits into little pieces for the base. Roll out the pastry and gently place it in the greased pie dish. Trim the edges by running the rolling pin over the dish and do fancy stuff with your fingers or a fork all around the edge. Sprinkle the apple cubes over the base, then fan out the sliced apples to form circles on top. In the centre arrange some slices like flower petals. Sprinkle with sugar and dot with butter so the tart caramelises in the oven. Bake at 125°C for one and a quarter hours. Remove from the oven and glaze with melted honey.

LUNCH WITH GERARD AND
JACQUELINE.

Jacqui set the table with the best silver and crystal, we cracked a
Sacred Hill Whitecliff Cabernet Rosé, perfect with a cold terrine, and
ate the products of our labour. We had made a leafy and herb salad
from Epicurean Supplies, Gerard had made some olive bread and
the *provençal* terrine was *vraiment très très bon* — light, colourful and
refreshing. We finished off with the apple tart, which had a very light
crust thanks to all the eggs and wasn't too sweet thanks to the
minimal addition of sugar. With the camera rolling Gerard said,

'Jacqui darling, you need a more plunging neckline.' The placid,
smokey-grey eyed Jacqui smiled.

'Gerard, please don't sell your wife. It's vulgar,' I said.

'Richard,' pleaded Jacqui, 'come and have something to eat. You
haven't eaten all day — I don't know how you cope.'

'It keeps me mean and lean,' Richard replied with a grin.

We finished filming on the Friday afternoon and my friends
Margs and Bill had kindly invited me to spend the
weekend with them in Havelock North. When I had first arrived in
Napier for the filming, Laurence and I had driven over to their place
to talk about their *crostini* operation. We discovered that they live in
the middle of nowhere.

'Isn't it interesting that all the people up here have the same surname on their letter boxes?' remarked Laurence.

'Yeah, and Herald Tribune is such an unusual name too,' I replied.

We finally found the house at the end of a long track and immediately decided to move in and live there for ever. A huge, square mansion made of brick and roughcast sat on a rise. The entrance was flanked by pillars, bougainvillaea and honeysuckle looking out over a wild garden full of dahlias, roses, agapanthas, lilies and daisies.

'If it needs looking after, it isn't in my garden,' said Margs to me later. 'I'm not the type to spend hours in the garden, so everything that grows there has strong survival skills.'

The front door was wide open, the dog greeted us amiably and no one was home. Being city people, Laurence and I were deeply impressed by the freedom of spirit required to go out and leave your house open. We permitted ourselves to sneak into the ground floor. On the left was the billiard room; on the right was the most divine drawing-room, again with the five windows and black, polished floors. It was full of Sanderson-covered sofas, old paintings and had a walnut table and grand piano. These rooms were like the bottom storeys of old palaces in Venice. The colours were opulently faded and they had a magnificent air of decadence. It was hot, the cicadas were singing; we stood smiling as if we were in a Somerset Maugham story. The only thing that was missing was the mint julep.

bill picked me up in their beat-up station wagon after the filming and our first stop was the liquor shop. I bought a couple of bottles of wine and Bill bought a carton of wine, whisky, gin, mixers, tomato juice.

'Are we expecting guests?' I asked.

'This is just for tonight,' he grinned. 'One wouldn't want to run out. One never knows what the future holds.'

'Quite right.'

They both come from farming families; in fact, Bill's parents' place was the farm but one next to Margs' parents and Margs has lived in this house all her life.

'We're not farmers,' laughed Margs. 'One day a steer fell into the swimming pool, which led to uncharitable reflections from the neighbours on Bill's farming skills.'

He is famous for his Bloody Marys, which can be offered to you at any time of the day from nine o'clock in the morning onwards. Whenever I mention this much loved couple to anyone, they inevitably ask, 'Did he make you a Bloody Mary?'

I slept in a room with a terrace looking out over the garden, swimming pool and tennis court and dreamed in a high, wooden bed with a blue-and-white duvet and white, lacy pillows. It was curiously restful to be able to sleep with the outside door open and not worry. Dog and cat hair everywhere. Margs and Bill are in love with their dogs who sleep on the bed with them. These dogs were treated like people and thought they were people and got crabby when I usurped their positions on the chairs. In the morning we rose late and I took myself on a tour of the rest of the house.

I am not a housey person, not seeing my lodgings as an extension of my ego, but this house enchanted me because although it was grand, it wasn't pretentious. I padded along the tongue-in-groove hallway with cross-battened ceiling to the big, double kitchen that had all sorts of mysterious, old-fashioned rooms off it like pantries, storerooms and little gardens full of herbs. The sitting-room had mushroom-pink walls, vases of orange flowers, book-lined walls and sporting prints. Down the other end of the house were more bedrooms and separate dressing-rooms for Margs and Bill, where the enigma of male and female grooming went on. On my outdoor excursion I discovered that the pool was overgrown and the tennis court unkempt, which only endeared me to the place more.

Breakfast was toast and tea, followed by whisky and milk, followed by Bill's question, 'When do I start making the Bloody Marys, darling?'

'Oh, wait till she's had her breakfast, darling.'

We were invited to lunch at Prue and Jamie's house — a short drive, said Margs. Just before Wellington (slight exaggeration) we got to their farm. Driving long distances to a lunch or a concert is nothing to country people, but how they ever get home is a puzzle to me. Prue was in the nursing class behind me at Auckland Hospital and is the only woman I have ever met who has a voice louder than mine. We sat on the vine-covered porch in rickety cane chairs and gazed at a huge copper beech and the garden overflowing with flowers.

'Jamie tried to kill that grapevine when we did the renovations on the porch,' said Prue brightly.

Beyond the porch was a pond and poplars and, in the near distance, the hills. On the left was a tennis court and on the right an old-fashioned, concrete swimming pool.

Pre-lunch drinks included culinary discussions with Jamie, who was nattily done out in black singlet, orange shirt, socks and old pants. This softly spoken, rural bodgie had hair like a hay stack, bushy eyebrows and stubbed his cigarettes out in a container that was either the sewing kit or an ashtray, I wasn't sure which, as it contained both butts and needles and thread.

'Peta,' he said, leaning back in his chair, 'I expect you missed out on the only real delicacy in these parts.'

'Mmm, I expect I did. You only find out the good stuff when the cameraman's gone home.'

'Yeah, well, do you know about mountain oysters and have you ever eaten lambs' tails?'

'Something tells me I'm about to find out all about it.'

'These things are best eaten in the spring during docking. You cut the lambs' tails off, chuck them in the embers of the fire and cook them till they scream,' he explained. 'Get hold of one end, pull the skin and wool off, sprinkle a bit of salt on and eat.'

Now I know why they drink in the Hawke's Bay.

'Gosh, and to think I wasted my time pratting around with wussy herbs,' I said.

Prue leaned over and told me that mountain oysters are sheep's testicles.

'Now, Peta,' said Jamie, warming to his subject, 'to get the balls, you bite them out of the living animal with your teeth or you extract them with your thumb and forefinger . . .'

'For Christ's sake, Jamie,' shouted Prue, 'she doesn't need to know all the bloody details.'

'And then you fry them in butter and onions — it's really a great delicacy.'

'Right! That's enough of that,' said Prue standing up, 'it's time for lunch.'

I smiled weakly at Margs and Bill whose placid faces revealed they were well accustomed to this genre of conversation.

We moved into the large kitchen that had ivy actually growing on the ceiling and sat down at a solid table for chicken, salad, wine and more stories. Prue is a vivacious, attractive woman with silver, curly hair who has very pretty daughters who look just like her. She ordered them around and they, smilingly, completely ignored her. Jamie smoked throughout the entire meal.

I strolled out through the dining-room with the huge, Art Deco, oak dining table and polished wooden floors into the ballroom-sized lounge with gold-embossed curtains, tatty furniture and grand piano. Jamie is a great hunter and fisher and there were trophies on the walls — animals' heads and such things and upstairs were the bedrooms, the master one being the size of a tennis court as they are in these old farm mansions. If Margs and Bill won't let me live in their house forever, this house would be my second choice.

That weekend the East Coast was blest with wild storms and driving rain, and as I sipped my Bloody Mary in front of Margs' fire, I felt deeply for the grape growers who I knew would be gnashing their teeth. Everyone was hoping for a good harvest after all that grape polishing, and as it turned out the rain didn't do as much damage as feared. It's now looking like the news is good and the winemakers don't have to get jobs at the meat works after all. This year, with the threat of rain, the grapes were harvested as soon as the

flavours were good, with no waiting around. Some Hawke's Bay winemakers are already declaring 1996 as the vintage of the decade for Chardonnay, but the general feeling seems to be that the quality will vary — there will be both outstanding and mediocre wines. In any case, my taste buds will be hanging out for whatever Sacred Hill has to offer.

just in case you want to get saucy, here's the recipe for Béarnaise Sauce:

BEARNAISE SAUCE

125 g (¹/₂ cup) WHITE WINE

2 tbsp TARRAGON VINEGAR

1 tbsp FINELY CHOPPED SHALLOTS

2 CRUSHED PEPPERCORNS

2 SPRIGS CHOPPED TARRAGON

1 SPRIG FINELY CHOPPED CHERVIL

1 SPRIG PARSLEY

3 EGG YOLKS

190 g (³/₄ cup) MELTED BUTTER

In a double boiler combine all the ingredients except the eggs and butter. Cook over a medium heat until reduced by half. Allow to cool slightly and, if you wish, strain off the herbs (though this is optional). With a beater or whisk, beat in the egg yolks, then slowly pour in the melted butter, beating all the time. The sauce should be smooth and thick and makes one and a quarter cups. Use to pour over grilled or broiled steak, fish, or eggs. Enjoy!